The ULTIMATE ZOMBIE EXERCISE & DIET BOOK

The ULTIMATE ZOMBIE EXERCISE & DIET BOOK

The Undead Guide to Health and Fitness

John Dixon

Illustrated by S. Kawai

Contents

Foreword

With the advent of the zombie pandemic in the first quarter of the 21st century, humans are facing their greatest crisis ever. With more than half the world's population either eaten or converted into mindless flesh-eating zombies, humans may soon become extinct.

Yet despite our impending destruction, the zombie has provided us with a unique opportunity to find new ways to improve our lives and our health.

What is the secret to the zombie success? What lessons can we learn from the zombie and apply to our own lives?   This book aims to answer these questions and more.

One of the greatest obstacles for people embarking on a new diet and fitness plan is confusion. There are so many diet plans and fitness routines to choose from - each championing the benefits of their particular method. The Zombie Exercise and Diet Plan bites through the confusion by providing you with a practical, low cost plan supported by scientific research.

Written by a natural health practitioner and zombie expert in collaboration with a top zombie beauty therapist, you will learn the health secrets of the zombie.

With practical advice and exciting new recipes from a top celebrity Zombie Eating Coach and author of the famous books – 'One Hundred and One Ways to Eat Oprah' and the 'Tasty Madonna Eating Guide', this book will educate you on the benefits of following the Zombie Plan.

In this book, you will learn about those bad human habits that weaken your body and how the zombie lifestyle is far superior. You will be taught exercises that zombies follow to keep in tip-top condition. Finally you will gain valuable zombie diet advice and tips in order to improve your digestion, increase your strength and provide you with the energy you need to fulfil your goals.

Introduction

Back to Basics

By the end of the 20th century, humans in Western society were experiencing unprecedented levels of prosperity. Earlier primitive man had been mostly concerned with the challenges of getting enough food, shelter and security. The world they lived in was harsh and full of dangers and their lifespan was short. As the human race progressed, they found solutions to these problems and made incredible advancements in farming, medicine, science and technology. Our lives became longer as food became plentiful and easily available in supermarkets. We made our homes cleaner and better insulated to protect us from the cold, with running water and electricity. We had inventions like the refrigerator, microwave oven and washing machine, which made life more convenient. We had more time for entertainment.

Yet in spite of this, at a time when humans should be congratulating themselves on their successes, doctor's waiting rooms and hospital beds are full. Self-help books are bestsellers. Diet pills are sold by the truckload and millions of people take prescription medicine every day for depression and many other health conditions. Diseases like cancer and heart disease have become prevalent along with addictions and obesity.

So what went wrong? As we step uncertainly into the future, many of us are looking back and wondering if in our quest to make our lives easier, we have not lost something that is essential to our health and wellbeing along the way.

In the West, many people will switch on the central heating every day in the winter and use air conditioning throughout the summer. They will drive instead of walk even for short distances and work at jobs which involve mostly sitting or standing. Recreational activities often involve passive activities like playing video games and watching TV. They will eat large amounts of nutritionally poor food - mostly refined carbohydrates, such as white bread, white rice and junk foods in large amounts with no concern over what's in it or who prepared it.

Earlier man would have grown or hunted their food. They would have seen where their food came from creating a more spiritual relationship with what they put in their mouth.

As we made our lives easier, we tended to become more passive and lazy. We believed that health and happiness should come to us and not the other way around.   In truth, we are not designed to live comfortable lives.

Primitive man hunting animals

For example, a labourer or a person who works outside is usually stronger and hardier than the average office worker who spends most of their time deskbound in an air-conditioned office. A person who works as a farmer, gardener or builder can work outside doing hard labour in the pouring rain without even getting a sniffle right up to the age of 80. Yet people with more inactive lives will often retire at 65 and die at 66 from various diseases. In truth it could be said that they died from boredom.

In reality, our bodies require daily physical activity. It needs exposure to the elements, dirt, bugs and animals. Hardship actually can make the body stronger. Our earliest ancestors understood the rule of 'survival of the fittest' and played by these rules.

The greatest strengths of the human have become their greatest weaknesses. With the many advancements in their lives, humans became first arrogant, complacent and then lazy. Unfortunately mother-nature is a cruel judge. While humans sat and enjoyed the easy life, nature threw up a new challenge to us in the form of the zombie plague.

Humans were unprepared for the zombie menace. Zombies attacked humans in the shopping centres, at schools and at their workplaces. So many humans were caught unprepared as they lay at home watching their plasma screen TVs, as zombies burst in and ate them. And those humans that were infected with the zombie virus, soon became zombies themselves.

Zombies hunting humans

Many people had difficulty in accepting the zombie phenomenon. They couldn't understand how a civilisation that had become so developed and so advanced could be challenged by something so primitive. They petitioned governments. They formed protest groups. They arranged charity concerts against the zombies. Unfortunately, they had forgotten how to deal with something as basic as a predator. Consequently they were eaten.

The zombie is the complete opposite to us. They live outside exposed to the elements. They hunt for their food like our primitive ancestors once did and they shun everything that makes our lives more comfortable. And in spite of our health food shops, our calorie controlled diets, our gym membership, our vitamin pills and exercise DVDs showing the latest fitness guru - the zombie has outperformed us and almost eradicated the human race.

So if we got it wrong, how can we get it right again? The Zombie Exercise and Diet Plan will help you with that, but before we embark on a new lifestyle plan, it is important to understand what we are doing wrong – our weaknesses and bad habits, so we can correct them and avoid them in the future. The next chapter looks at the factors that brought down the human race and are responsible for making us fat, unhealthy and tired.

Chapter 1

The Problem of Plenty

Diseases of affluence

One of the greatest paradoxes to affect human-kind in the 21st century are that while amazing advancements have been made in the fields of science, education, technology, hygiene and medicine - certain diseases have actually increased because of these improvements. In the past, humans were afflicted by diseases caused by poverty, malnutrition and poor sanitation. Scourges like tuberculosis, smallpox, polio and the plague killed many. In modern times, thanks to vaccinations, hygiene, sanitation and medicines such as antibiotics - many of these diseases have nearly been eradicated. People are living longer.

Unfortunately, as our lives became more comfortable, we have become more susceptible to other diseases. For example, certain cancers, type-2 diabetes, asthma, coronary heart disease, obesity, allergies, inflammatory bowel disease along with mental conditions like depression and alcoholism have actually increased. Heart disease and cancer were the number one and two killers of humans prior to the zombie outbreak.

So what is the cause of all this? Let's explore some of the factors.

Less strenuous activity

As humans use motor vehicles, they lose an opportunity to exercise their legs, lungs and heart. It is not unusual to see humans drive to places within easy walking distance and to shun small chances of exercise by using escalators and elevators to the first or second floor.

Many modern jobs involve little or no physical labour leading to irregular exercise. Office workers, drivers and security guards will typically spend eight to ten hours sitting down and breathing poor air. Children and students spend hours sitting in classrooms and lecture rooms. Recreation often involves sitting in front of the TV, computer or games consoles. All of this leads to prolonged periods of inactivity, which weakens the muscles. The consequences of this, is that the human body becomes weak and less resilient. There is less exposure to infectious agents and 'real' stresses against the body like scratches, cuts and parasites, which allows less chance for the immune system to be exercised. The immune system then starts to over-react to harmless substances in the body causing allergies and possibly autoimmune diseases.

Easy availability of inferior foods

Food is medicine, yet it can also be poison. Affluent human societies have easy accessibility to large amounts of low cost, high calorie food. Supermarkets sell tonnes of commercially prepared, processed foods focused on sales and profit. They sell refined foodstuffs such as white bread, white rice and white noodles, candies, high fat and high sugar foods at very low costs which are not fresh. Due to their high sugar content, these foods can make us fat and have other negative effects on the body, which we will talk about later.

Worse of all, this food requires less physical exertion in order to obtain it, which would have been able to offset the negative aspects of it. A hundred years ago, humans may have walked miles to the local shop or market. Thousands of years ago, they would have hunted an animal or spent hours fishing. Nowadays, a human will drive up to the supermarket, push a trolley around and comfortably pick their food off the shelves without working up a sweat.

When the zombie outbreak occurred, one of the first actions taken by humans was to raid the local supermarkets. They searched for long-lasting tinned and processed foods, with the intention of holding up until the crisis ended. Soon, the supermarkets became empty and even these inferior foods were no longer available.

Old skills like protecting land and growing vegetables, which kept our earlier ancestors alive had been long forgotten. People know how to eat, but not how to make food anymore. As people grew hungry, their strength diminished making them easy targets for the zombie.

Modern diets are full of sugary and processed foods

Greater use of alcohol and tobacco

In moderation and in social situations, alcohol and tobacco are enjoyable social drugs. Unfortunately, if taken in large amounts they have negative effects on the body. Alcohol is high in calories. It also causes an increase in appetite as meals appear tastier when consumed with alcohol. When alcohol passes the liver, a by-product called acetate is formed, which inhibit the fat burning capabilities of the body. Both these factors can result in weight gain.

Smoking causes a lot of free radicals. Free radicals are unstable atoms with an odd number of electrons causing them to damage other healthy tissues. Smoking depletes vitamin C, which is needed to protect your body from infection and maintain healthy bones. Both smoking excessively and alcoholism is associated with diseases like liver disease and lung cancer.

Stress

Stress is an important part of life and can be positive. The human body is designed to deal with stress. It keeps the body alert and able to avoid danger. Unfortunately, modern day living can be stressful in a negative way. The scientist Hans Selye showed the negative effects of stress with his model called the General Adaptive Syndrome (GAS). In his work, he subjected laboratory rats to stress. Many of them became very sick - suffering intestinal ulcers, wasting away of the thymus and enlargement of the adrenal glands.

In the general adaptive syndrome (GAS), the body goes through three stages when dealing with stress: Alarm, Resistance and Recovery or Exhaustion. In the 'alarm' stage, a stress appears - for example a crazed zombie jumps out and threatens to eat you. This triggers the 'fight or flight' response. The body prepares for action by releasing stress hormones – adrenaline, cortisol and norepinephrine into the blood stream which puts us into an 'attack' state. These hormones have amazing effects: our breathing rate increases, blood moves away from our digestive system into our muscles, our eyesight sharpens and our impulses become quicker as we prepare to deal with the zombie. These changes require a lot of energy.

This response continues during the 'resistance' stage as we contend with the zombie by hitting it with a hard object or running from it. All our energy is focused on dealing with the danger. It is always better to deal with this danger quickly, as a prolonged conflict can be exhausting.

Finally when we have killed the zombie or escaped from it, we enter the 'recovery' stage where the body returns to a state of calm.   However, if the body is not allowed to recover and instead experiences continual stress (also known as distress), the 'exhaustion' stage occurs. Too much distress can lead to 'burnout'.

As an attack from a wild zombie can be resolved quickly, the human is able to recover from these effects without harm. Unfortunately, the same stress response occurs almost daily among modern humans in situations that are not life threatening. For example, when a boss shouts at us in the workplace, we have to grit our teeth and listen. Or when there is a signalling fault on a crowded subway train during rush hour and we have to stand and wait crushed against other sweaty people. Or when a final reminder for a bill comes in and we can't afford to pay it. All these situations create the stress response which unfortunately cannot be dealt with immediately. Instead we must suppress our natural stress reaction.

The long term effects of stress begin to drain the body causing wear and tear. This can cause headaches, stomach ulcers, constipation, cardiovascular disease, asthma, depression, anxiety and sleep problems. Stress also inhibits digestion causing weight gain and depletes the body of many vitamins and minerals necessary for healthy function. Many humans use tobacco or cigarettes to relieve the stress but actually this creates more tension in the body and depletes our body further.

The worst effects are on the immune system. The immune system produces white blood cells: T-lymphocytes that protect the body from bacteria, infections, cancer cells and also *tries* to protect us from the zombie virus. High levels of stress suppress these T-lymphocytes, which weakens the immune system and makes the body more vulnerable to infections and colds.

We take longer to recover from them and experience much worse symptoms. Unsurprisingly, under these circumstances, the zombie virus had no problem in taking over our weakened immune systems and turning many humans into zombies very quickly.

So stress makes you sick, tired and overweight.   It goes without saying, that zombies are not troubled with stress. They have a healthy stress response. Actually, the best way to cool down the 'fight or flight' response is to give the body what it wants. The body is prepared for physical activity, so that's exactly what we should do. If we do vigorous exercise to the point of sweating, we metabolize excess stress hormones and also release endorphins – hormones that lift the mood and make us physically and mentally calmer. This is one of the keystones of the Zombie Exercise Plan.

In Chapter Four we will look at the perfect zombie exercises to help us deal with the negative effects of stress.

Workplace stress

Jim's Testimony

"I had a very stressful job in the city at a big investment firm. The salary was very high with many perks but I had to work long hours (sometimes all night) and was continually pressured by my boss every day. I suffered insomnia, drank wine and beer excessively and my blood pressure was very high. Eventually the daily meetings and deadlines became too much for me and I started having panic attacks. It was then that I started the Zombie Exercise and Diet Plan. It was a hard choice at first, but I decided to give it a go.

The first thing I did was to hunt down and eat my boss. Then I ate some of my annoying co-workers. It was amazing; my stress immediately disappeared and for the first time I could think clearly about my life goals. I decided to quit my job and set up my own business as a full time Zombie Fitness and Diet Coach. A lot of my clients are corporate city workers and the best thing is that I probably earn more money now doing something that I love".

Jim Porter, Zombie Fitness and Diet Coach

Chapter 2
Enter the Zombie

The zombie

Before the onset of the zombie pandemic, the zombie was considered a quaint folklore originating among African descendants in Haiti and from tales in the North Mbundu language of Angola, who referred to them as 'zonbi' and 'nzumbe' respectively. Traditionally, the zombie is an animated corpse which has been resurrected back to life using an ancient magic called 'vodou' or 'voodoo' by a sorcerer or 'bokor'. Once resurrected, the will of the zombie is under complete control of the sorcerer. In many cases, the sorcerer would use a mix of psychotropic drugs to hypnotize humans and turn them into mindless slaves. Due to the effects of these compounds, these 'zombie' slaves may take on the appearance of being dead, but in some cases they were still alive.

A similar story exists in China where the re-animated corpse is called a 'jiang shi'. Families who could not afford to transport deceased family members back to their home town for burial, would pay for Taoist monks called 'Corpse Walkers' to resurrect the corpse and teach them to hop back themselves at night. The jiang shi may also kill people to absorb their life essence.

The modern day zombie is a lot different to these traditional stories. Today's zombies are truly *undead*. There are no drugs involved and no sorcerer to control them. In fact the modern day zombie retains his will and chooses an independent course of life of hunting and eating humans.

The source of the zombie virus is still a mystery to modern scientists, who have been unable to identify the exact structure of it. Some theories suggest that it is a mutated form of the encephalitis or rabies virus. Conspiracy theorists say it is an alien virus or a government-made biological weapon. A few scientists postulate that it may have been a mutation of human antibodies in response to a new cancer vaccine that had been tested on humans prior to the zombie breakout. Western countries often blame the origin of the zombie virus on China or the African continent, whereas people in Africa and in China consider the North American continent responsible. Whatever the cause, the zombie outbreak swiftly swept across the world.

The zombie virus is a blood borne disease. It can be spread if the saliva or blood of an infected person enters an uninfected person. It is not airborne, although if an infected person coughs sputum into the face of someone who then swallows it or if it enters the eye then that person can become infected.

The incubation period often varies from four to six hours. If the physical condition of the person is quite bad

- for example, they were severely ravaged in the initial zombie attack – then symptoms may begin in as little as two hours. The initial symptoms will usually be fever and headaches although on occasion there may sometimes be myalgia (muscle aches) and sweating. Even though the temperature will be high, the infected person will often complain of chills and ask for more blankets. There will also be nausea and tiredness. These symptoms will gradually increase in severity ending in sudden death after ten hours. In other instances, the person may suffer from hallucinations and fall into a coma. Death will often occur during this comatose state within the next two to five hours.

The onset of death heralds the next stage of the zombie virus – 'the resurrection'. The 'death' itself may last on average about ten to twenty minutes although there have been some cases of it lasting for up to four hours. After this, brain impulses suddenly start firing in the brain causing a re-activation of the body and then resurrection occurs. The zombie comes back to life, usually with little to no recollection of its previous life.

One of the side-effects experienced during the transformation from *life*-to-*death*-to-*undeath* is impaired brain function. During death, respiration ceases – the person stops breathing and oxygen is not transported to the brain. If the brain is without oxygen for more than four minutes, permanent cell death occurs. Consequently when the zombie reanimates, large portions of its brain are damaged and cannot function.

Fortunately, the zombie virus appears to protect the hindbrain, also known as the reptilian brain, which governs our primal instincts - hunger, survival, respiration and heartbeat and our most basic autonomous functions including movement. Most of the other higher-function brain areas responsible for emotion, reason and thought are badly damaged or destroyed. This is one of the reasons why when a zombie is re-animated, he immediately wants to eat flesh. Basically he is trying to satisfy his most basic primeval desire.

There is also the problem with rigor mortis - a chemical reaction occurring in the body where the limbs become stiff and difficult to move. It usually starts about three to four hours after death. Rigor mortis begins in the eyelids, neck and jaw and occurs in the other muscles and internal organs. As most zombies tend to resurrect long before then, they are generally not affected by rigor mortis. However there may still be some minor effects. In cases where there is a delayed resurrection, the zombie may be very stiff for about the next twelve hours. However, the effects will pass after about forty eight hours and the zombie will start to loosen up after this time. Zombies often use the various muscle loosening exercises and stretches as shown in this book to relieve the effects of rigor mortis more quickly.

Other cell damage to various systems and parts of the body also occurs, hence there is a greater requirement for nutrition especially protein in order to repair the damage. As humans are a rich source of all the nutrients that zombies require, this is the reason why zombies are solely preoccupied with hunting and eating them.

Zombie physiology

As human science does not yet fully acknowledge the concept of 'the resurrection of life after death', classifying the zombies has been a difficult and confusing issue and the subject of much debate among scientists and academics.

Zombies are physiologically identical to humans. They have limbs, a torso, sense organs, skin and hair. The internal organs and systems of the body are the same. Yet, there are some fundamental differences. Humans are alive, whereas zombies are technically speaking 'deceased'. They have experienced the process known as 'dying' and physiological tests indicate that their bodies are in a very slow but steady state of decay. Yet, they are still able to move and carry out basic functions, which indicates that they are still alive.

In order to move the debate forward as to what to call the zombie phenomenon, a new term of classification was adopted. The zombies come to be referred to as the 'un-dead' or 'living dead'.

Research into the zombie phenomenon is an ongoing process, but some things are known about zombies. Contrary to popular belief, zombies do breathe air, although their requirement for oxygen is significantly lower. It is apparent that zombies can survive for long periods without the need for oxygen demonstrated by their ability to survive underwater, but it is not clear how long they can survive. Zombies also do have a faint heartbeat. Their heart still pumps oxygenated and deoxygenated blood around their body.

Zombie blood is quite viscous containing a large amount of fibrinogen and blood clotting factor, so their blood clots very quickly when injured. Some tests have shown that as the zombie virus multiplies and reaches a peak level of infection in the body – open wounds will start clotting. It is thought that this is an *'intelligent'* function of the virus to protect its zombie host. For example, a human may be badly savaged in an initial zombie attack and bleed profusely. If the bleeding carried on indefinitely, the newly resurrected zombie would be too weak and unable to move. It would be quite a hindrance to the zombie if it suffered from the effects of anaemia. As a result of this function, a zombie may not bleed excessively when attacked unless an artery is cut. For example, if the head or arm is chopped off with a samurai sword, it is quite typical for blood to come spewing out like a geyser.

A zombie's brain function is impaired. Pain receptors do not register any messages with the brain, meaning that a zombie does not feel pain ever. The zombie immune system is still the subject of much study and much is not yet known.   It is hypothesised that the zombie virus itself is able to destroy any infectious agents - bacteria, viruses or fungi that enter the body and would contribute to quicker deterioration. A lot of energy is directed into the limbs and intestines and stomach resulting in a large appetite and increased levels of activity. As zombies are in a state of decay, they tend to smell quite bad so it is quite important they have a shower after working out.

The zombie pandemic

When zombies first appeared in the first quarter of the 21st century, the zombie virus spread relentlessly through all the small towns, cities, countries and eventually all the continents of the planet. There was no stopping it. A single bite or scratch from a zombie would spread the virus to a new host. Within hours that person would be dead and reawaken as a zombie. The zombie appetite for human flesh was insatiable. Zombies hunted in packs eating men and women, young and old. They didn't discriminate between looks, social status, religion or race. They would eat anybody, even pets and politicians.

In the beginning, humans still had the advantage. We had organised structures such as the police and army with their weapons, tanks and jets. Yet despite our best efforts, the zombies persevered and increased in numbers. Eventually they reached a breakthrough point and outnumbered humans.

Regrettably, in the modern world we have lost the ability to deal with problems by ourselves. Instead of picking up a shovel or golf club and attacking them, many of us cowered at home waiting for the government to fix the problem. Unfortunately, many governments applied ineffective strategies, such as setting up expensive commissions to *look* into the problem and creating the notorious 'Zombie Tax'. Perhaps instead, we should have been learning from the zombie's self-determination and relentless pursuit of their personal goals - then things might have turned out differently.

Killing zombies is extremely difficult. Zombies can withstand knife attacks, shootings (except to the head), baseball bat blows and poison. In contrast, most humans are not trained in hand-to-hand combat or the use of weapons. Many humans have poor levels of fitness. Even fewer have the actual physical and psychological experience of killing (gained from killing animals), which is necessary to destroy zombies. Consequently, zombies soon surpassed humans and became top of the food chain.

So what is the zombie secret? What sets them apart from humans and what can we learn from them in order to improve our health and fitness? In the next chapter we will look at the advantages of the zombie lifestyle compared to humans.

Humans are often ineffective against zombie attacks

Frank's Testimony

"My ex-wife used to nag me all the time. She found fault with everything I did and always compared me to the neighbours who seemed to be so much better. My wife expected me to keep up with them. I had to buy a new car, a new kitchen unit, wood panelled flooring and a holiday to the Bahamas. I only had a modest salary and soon I was in deep credit card debt. I became very stressed and couldn't see a way to deal with my problems. I went to my local bar every night and lost even more money playing online gambling.

And then, I saw an infomercial for the Zombie Plan late at night and decided to give it a go. The first thing I had to do was take full responsibility for my predicament. I had to identify the areas of my life that were causing me problems and tackle them head on.

My first action was to eat my neighbours so my wife wouldn't be able to compare me to them anymore. I knew I needed to do more and so I ate her expensive little poodle. It was immensely satisfying. Finally, I ate my wife. Amazingly, all my outgoings dropped by seventy percent.

I'm now so much happier following the plan and I am getting my finances back under control. I've also started dating a lady at my local Zombie Exercise and Diet Club. Our values are compatible and we plan to get married next year".

Frank Cooper, Business consultant

Chapter 3

Benefits of the Zombie Lifestyle

This chapter looks at aspects of the zombie lifestyle and explores how zombies are not hindered by certain lifestyle and eating habits that are disadvantageous to humans.

Zombies eat free-range

Humans eat low quality mass-produced meat and it makes them slow, sluggish and sick. Curiously, very few humans are conscious that their meat is of such poor quality. This may be the reason why zombies were able to eat so many of us so quickly. Ninety percent of the meat found in supermarkets, fast food shops and restaurants are factory farmed meats. The main meats that humans like to eat are chicken, pork and beef.

Thousands of chickens are held in battery cages - where usually four to five chickens are held in a small cage and are given artificial light only. Pigs are held in pens side-by-side with hundreds of other pigs. Dairy cows are intensely milked and mass farmed to provide meat for fast-food hamburger chains. Close confined spaces lead to animals cannibalising each other.

These animals are fed low quality feed. In some cases the ground-up remains of other animals from the same species are fed back to them. Although filling and cheap, these foods are of inferior quality containing large amounts of steroids, antibiotics and stress hormones in their blood. Many are contaminated by faeces along with E coli and Campylobacter bacteria due to the development of antibiotic resistant strains in reaction to overuse of antibiotics.

Zombies prefer to avoid such foods. They prefer their meats free-range. Humans that are allowed to move about freely in open space and exercise their limbs in natural sunlight taste better and are more wholesome.

Free-range humans have generally consumed a wider variety of diet - minerals and vitamins and have higher levels of vitamin A and omega 3 fatty acids, which are more nourishing to zombies. Free-range humans also have lower levels of saturated fat and there is less risk of unnecessary antibiotic or steroid consumption.

Warning

Although humans who eat large amounts of factory farmed foods are often easier to catch due to poorer health and fitness levels, it is important to be wary of eating humans who have ingested large amounts of these foods because of the toxins they contain. It is far more beneficial to eat humans with natural diets and who live in a more natural environment. Farmers and fishermen are highly recommended. Some athletes may be an acceptable alternative

Zombies don't drink mineral water

The most recent fad for humans is bottled water. Thousands of bottles are thrown away in landfill or incinerated each year. On any warm day, it is not unusual to see joggers, yoginis or fashion-conscious humans carrying bottles of mineral or spring water regardless of whether they feel real thirst or not. Due to successful advertising campaigns, bottle water has become a fashion accessory.

Yet they can be lethal. In the first zombie outbreak, many young ladies and joggers were easily eaten by zombies. By clutching onto their bottles of water they only had one hand free to push off a zombie attack. Sadly, it was not enough.

Suffice to say zombies don't drink water. They don't need to. The human body is made up of about sixty percent water. It's contained in the blood and the body tissues. When a zombie eats a human, he gets all the water he needs.

Zombies eat raw

It is well known that zombies eat a 100% raw carnivorous diet. This way of eating, also known as 'raw foodism' has several advantages over cooked meals. Zombies believe that cooked foods (cooked over 40 degrees Celsius) have lost a lot of their nutritional value and can be harmful to the body. Raw foods contain natural enzymes – proteins, which are important in building the body's cells. Enzymes are destroyed in the heating process. Even some traditional human diets involve eating primarily raw meats and organ meats: as practiced by some Aboriginal tribes, the Nenet tribe of Siberia and the Inuit people. With the benefits of these enzymes, zombies enjoy a far more efficient digestion than the majority of humans.

In a work called Nutrition and Physical Degeneration, Weston A. Price observed dental degeneration of the teeth of second generations who removed raw foods from their diet. It is believed that digestive enzymes like proteases and lipases, which are present in raw foods help digestion. These enzymes are destroyed by heating over 40 degrees Celsius.

For humans, one problem with eating raw food is the greater risk of food poisoning. Heating does have the benefit of killing bacteria and some parasites. Many humans have suffered from gastroenteritis from eating raw foods. Therefore when following the Zombie Diet, it is advisable to avoid meats that have spoiled.

Incidentally, it is believed that the zombie virus neutralises most toxic substances that enter the body.

Zombies eat vegetarians

Some humans, otherwise known as 'vegetarians', abstain from eating meat, fish, seafood or eggs. These foods are high in proteins, which are an important nutrient for the body. As an alternative, vegetarians prefer to obtain their protein from plant-based foods like tofu, pulses, dairy and certain vegetables. Such diets are considered to be healthy leading to reduced cases of heart disease and certain types of cancer, partly due to the reduced amount of saturated fats.

Suffice to say, zombies are not vegetarian. Due to the need for high levels of nutrients to repair their decaying bodies, their recommended daily allowance of protein is far higher than the average human. It would be impossible for them to obtain even a third of their needed protein intake from a vegetarian source. However zombies will quite happily eat vegetarians, especially if they feel the need to detox their bodies after eating a lot of rich, high saturated fatty human meats.

Warning

Some vegetarians eat too many carbohydrates and suffer from vitamin and mineral deficiencies due to the lack of complete protein in their diet. Vegetarians may be at risk of osteoporosis (calcium deficiency), anaemia (iron deficiency) and tiredness due to B vitamin deficiency.

Zombies should be wary of eating vegetarians as they may not get all the nutrients they require. When following the zombie diet, it may be advisable to avoid Buddhist or yoga centres where vegetarians are often prevalent.

Zombies practice fasting

As strange as it sounds, zombies carry out this ancient practice. Humans are not easy to catch and it can be many hours, days or even weeks before a zombie is able to find a fresh human to eat. This requires a zombie to go for long periods of time without feeding. Yet despite this, a zombie will still have enough energy to run after and subdue a human.

Fasting is the act of abstaining from food or drink (or both) for a period of time usually 24 hours, but sometimes for several days. It is regularly practiced in several religions. There has been research to suggest that there are health benefits to caloric restriction such as reduced risks of cancer, cardiovascular disease, diabetes and auto-immune disorders.

Proponents of fasting believe it can rest the digestive system and allow for detoxification of the body. A modified version of fasting is called 'intermittent fasting', which is a pattern of eating that alternates between periods of fasting and non-fasting. This involves missing meals at times. For example, you may miss breakfast or only have one meal a day at night. It is believed that during fasting, the stimulant hormones – catecholamines are released which improves mental focus. Fasting also allows blood sugar levels to be kept more stable. Fasting is not recommended for young people or children as their bodies are still growing and they need lots of nutrients for growth.

Zombies don't waste their food

Humans throw away almost a hundred million tonnes of food every year. Households, restaurants and supermarkets waste 50% of the food that is produced. Supermarkets, grocery stores and restaurants routinely throw away food in perfectly good condition if they are close to their sell-by-date, even though they are still edible. They also routinely throw away foods with slightly damaged packaging. And instead of recycling this food or passing it onto other hungry humans, most of this food ends up in landfill or is incinerated at waste disposal plants.

Humans are also very picky about what they eat. If a food is not ascetically pleasing they may throw it away. When consuming animal flesh, they will often only eat the muscle areas and discard the rest, especially the offal, which is far more nutritious than muscle protein. Many humans seem to have food sensitivities and are intolerant to gluten and dairy.   Curiously, in less affluent countries, fewer people suffer from these kinds of food sensitivities.

In contrast, zombies believe in the philosophy of 'waste not, want not'. They are efficient eaters and absolutely hate wasting food. A pack of zombies will strip a human to bones in minutes, eating every edible part of the human - the brain, eyes, blood, lips and skin. Even the inedible parts will be munched upon. Zombies will happily suck on the bones for a few hours afterwards to suck out the marrow for the nutrients.

Zombies chew their food

Chewing is an essential part of digestion. The process of digestion begins before we even eat the food. For example, when a zombie sees or smells a human nearby, the brain sends signals to his digestive organs; his stomach starts secreting digestive fluids and the zombie starts drooling and produces saliva. This prepares the body for its meal of human flesh.

It is then the role of the digestive system to turn a mouthful of flesh (protein) into smaller amino acids so they can be easily used by the body. The process is carried out by stomach acid in the stomach, which breaks the food into a proteinous soup, which then passes into the small intestines to be absorbed by the micro villa on the lining of our intestinal walls. The question of whether this action can be a short efficient process or a long laborious process is decided in our mouth. If we chew our food into smaller particles, it can be more easily broken down and the nutrients and energy absorbed. If we *wolf* the food down in large gulps, the chances are that pound of flesh will sit heavily in the stomach for hours causing indigestion.

A zombie chews his food thoroughly. If you watch a zombie eating a freshly caught human, you will see that he chews with relish - opening and closing his mouth in almost a meditative trance. The benefits speak for themselves – zombies are able to efficiently utilize all the energy in the flesh they eat. They don't have problems with flatulence or acid reflux and have higher energy levels.

When you embark on the zombie diet, it is a good idea to chew each mouthful of flesh about twenty-five to thirty times. Try eating with your mouth open and listen to the sound of bones crunching and fat squelching. It can be very soothing.   It can also be a good idea to listen to relaxing music while you eat to aid with digestion.

Zombies don't watch TV

The average human watches five hours of TV per day. That means that in one year, you may have spent seventy-six days watching TV. Although TV has some educational value and can teach us many things about the world, most of the time it is irrelevant. Many shows are simply 'filler', such as reality shows, soap operas, sensationalist news channels and nearly *all* daytime TV programming. A large amount of TV time is designated to commercials to advertise products that we do not need. Often TV provides nothing of real value to our lives and ultimately steals our time.

It has been said that TV is the 'opiate of the masses'. TV has a hypnotic effect on the senses. When we watch TV, our brain activity switches from the left hemisphere (the logical side) over to the right hemisphere (the emotional side). There is also a release of endorphins (feel-good chemicals), which have a sedative-type effect on the brain similar to taking an opiate drug. This means that TV is addictive. Furthermore, when a heavy TV watcher stops watching TV, they can suffer from withdrawal symptoms such as depression, anxiety and irritability. Due to its hypnotic effects, people often overeat whilst watching TV. Our brains are not engaged and we are not aware when our stomachs are full. It's quite common to snack excessively on salty and sweet foods. An excess of these foods can cause obesity and other diseases.

TV can even kill you. According to some research, watching more than four hours of TV a day leads to an 80% increased risk of death from cardiovascular disease and a 40% increase of risk of all causes of death compared to people who watch less than two hours of TV a day. This is irrespective of diet, exercise or smoking. So even if you eat a good diet, exercise regularly and don't smoke or drink, watching more than four hours a day can kill you just as certainly as a zombie.

In order to use our muscles, we contract and relax them during movement. This muscle contraction is important for body metabolism - especially converting glucose to energy and the metabolism of cholesterol (a fatty substance in the blood). So it is important not to be too sedentary and slump for hours in front of the screen. This does not mean that sitting excessively is bad for us. If we sit upright with good posture or do some stretching whilst watching TV, we can actually get a good workout during the time we do want to watch TV.

The zombies never watch TV. Their brain hemispheres are no longer stimulated by those flickering images. They are not imprisoned by this weak drug and in this regard they have surpassed human consciousness. Watching TV makes our brains sluggish and our bodies weak. In all the hours wasted watching TV we could have been conditioning our bodies or learning new survival and fighting skills to face the zombie menace. Instead we became their TV meal.

TV reduces our attention levels

Zombies don't have gym membership

Tim's Testimony

"I was an avid gym-goer for years. I would go twice a week and do the same workout - twenty minutes on the treadmill followed by some lifting on the weight machines. Sometimes I'd join the spinning classes. I really thought I was in reasonable shape.

I'd heard about the Zombie Exercise and Diet Plan from some of my friends but I was so stuck in doing my usual workout routine, I just dismissed them.

Then one day there was a zombie outbreak at the gym. Those zombies were savage. They tore right through all the muscleheads. Pretty soon one little old zombie lady got me in her sights and grabbed me. I tried to push her off, but it was as if she had superhuman strength. I couldn't believe how strong she was. I realised then, that my way of exercising had not been effective".

Tim Jones, deceased

The concept of health and fitness among humans is based more on vanity then reality. This may be due to the fashion and Hollywood movie industry, where fitness has come to be considered synonymous with big muscles for a man or a slim, size eight body for a female. Zombies train naturally. Large muscles may seem impressive or intimidating, but functionally they are not as strong as they appear. For example, a person may be able to bench-press a hundred and fifty pounds, but may not be able to do one single pull up. Big heavy muscles can be cumbersome and cause the human to be slower making them an easy target for a group of biting zombies. Slim women also can lack strength making them ineffective against zombie attacks.

Zombies don't need expensive weight-lifting equipment or running machines. They don't watch exercise videos with the latest fitness guru. The zombie fitness plan is based on functional fitness. Zombies focus on natural strength-building, bodyweight exercises such as push ups, free weight squats, handstands and pull ups. They exercise their heart and lungs and overall strength by combining intense activity coupled with cardio exercises. Zombies will also do long-distant walking in order to build up stamina. They train for agility by climbing up buildings and crawling through sewers. They practice resistance training by wading through rivers and pools.

The result is a lean strong zombie body that is able to punch and kick through boarded up windows and doors. They can wrestle humans larger than themselves, tear off flesh with their bare hands and break bones.

In the next chapter, we will see some of these exercises in detail, with instructions on how to make them part of your daily practice.

Jenny's Testimony

"I was a teacher in an inner-city comprehensive school. The children were badly disciplined and unruly and I had to deal with 'monster parents', who blamed me for their children's lack of progress. I was stressed and became very depressed. Every evening, I would collapse in front of the TV and binge on cake. At work, I would sit at my desk all day and snack on chocolates. My weight ballooned to a size 18 and the kids and the other faculty started making fun of me. I was desperately unhappy and that was when I decided to try the Zombie Exercise and Diet Plan.

At first it was difficult, but I soon discovered the joy in this way of life. When the bad kids played up, I ate them - bones and all. Then I ate their horrible parents, when they came to complain. And finally I really got a great work-out hunting and ripping the flesh off the other teachers in the school corridors. I even ate the janitor.

Now I am a size 10. I have lots of energy and my stress has all but gone. The best thing about doing this plan was that I was able to save a fortune on grocery shopping as there was an abundant supply of children at my school".

Miss Jenny Boyles, teacher

Chapter 4

Zombie exercises

Functional fitness is an important component of the zombie exercise programme. This is made up of five categories:

- The 'warm up' - to prepare the body and loosen the joints.

- 'Stretching' – to increase flexibility and optimize body functioning.

- 'Strength building' - vigorous exercises that create real strength: the kind of strength that enables a zombie to rip an arm off a human.

- 'Stamina building' - which enables a zombie to chase after a human for hours without getting tired.

- Finally, we show the 'quiet down' exercises that calm the body after the workout and build *internal* strength.

Warm up

The warm-up exercises may appear simple, but they are absolutely essential. These basic exercises, if carried out daily over years can gently strengthen and loosen the joints helping with conditions like arthritis. For the elderly and people in a weak state, the warm ups can be done by themselves as a complete training program until their strength gradually increases. Zombies often use them to rehabilitate their bodies after injury.

Head rolls

This exercise stretches the muscles of the neck, upper shoulder, back and chest. Tightness in these muscles can cause neck and jaw pain and headaches. This exercise should be done in a gentle circular motion, whilst breathing in and out in a smooth co-ordinated movement.

- Stand or sit straight with your arms by your side.

- Breathe in and gently drop your head forward so your chin is touching your chest. You will feel a stretch in the back of your neck.

- Breathe in and gently circle your head to the right so your ear almost brushes past your shoulder. Keep breathing and circle it to the back opening up the front of your neck.

- Breathe out and continue rotating to the left and round to the front position again.

- Continue three more times and then change direction for four times.

Head rolls

Circling the waist

This exercise gently warms up and stretches the waist, abdomen, lower back and opens up the hip and upper legs. It strengthens the back muscles and can prevent lower back pain when you get older.

- Stand with legs shoulder-width apart. Put your hands on your hips.

- Push your hips to the front.

- Breathe in and move your hips in a circle to the right and then round to the back pushing your bottom out.

- As you breathe out, keep circling to the left and to the front again.

- Breathe in and repeat three more times. Then reverse direction for four more times.

Circling the waist

Circle the knees

The knees are a joint that need to support the weight of the whole body. Being overweight puts a lot of pressure on this area. These exercises gently strengthen the knees and prevent against knee pain.

- Stand with both feet close together. Gently bend your knees bringing your hips lower and put your hands on your knees.

- Breathe in and in a smooth circular motion, move your knees to the right and to the back. Breathe out and circle to the left and to the front again.

- Repeat three more times and change directions for four rotations in the opposite direction.

The lower back and knees are related areas of the body, where people feel weakness or pain more often. They are also areas which are put under a lot of pressure when we lift heavy weights. The benefits of the Zombie Exercise Plan are that these parts of the body are treated with sensitivity and gradually strengthened.

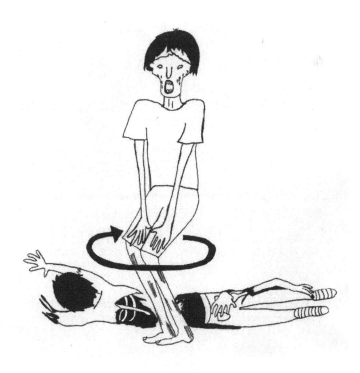

Circle the knees

Reach for the sky

If you've ever seen a cat stretch its whole body when it wakes up, this exercise has a similar effect. It enlivens your entire spine, arms and legs.

- Stand with feet shoulder-width apart or close together.

- Take a deep breath and as you breathe out, reach your arms to the sky and stretch.

- Hold for thirty seconds and release. Repeat as many times as you want.

You want to stretch the spine and open up the space between each vertebra. People who sit down a lot slumped at desks or in front of computers will have vertebrae that are closed tight together and paraspinal muscles that are weak. The spinal column houses an important network of nerves and blood vessels. If these are contracted together, their functioning is hindered making us operate less effectively.

When you stretch, use your imagination as though an invisible thread is pulling you up into the universe whilst your feet are being pulled to the centre of the earth.

Reach for the sky

Standing forward bend

Stretches the muscles of the back and hamstrings.

- Stand with legs shoulder-width apart.

- Take a deep breath and as you breathe out, gently bend forward from the hips to reach for the floor. Keep your legs straight.

- You want to just relax into the stretch - don't force it. Just hang. Breathe normally for one to three minutes and gently return to the original position.

This exercise is one of the easiest in this book. It requires almost no energy to perform. Instead you are using the power of the Earth's magnetic core to do all the work for you. Allow the power of gravity to pull your torso down further. Just focus on keeping your legs straight. When you come out of the stretch, you may feel your spine feels longer and you are taller. Appreciate this feeling for a few moments as an indication of how different your body would feel if these muscles were more open.

Standing forward bend

Stretching

Stretching has many benefits. It increases the range of motion and flexibility, which also promotes blood circulation. In tight areas, the muscles are constricted and there may be knots. The circulation of nutrients and waste products in the blood are hindered, meaning that the body cannot operate at its optimum efficiency. You can get tired more easily and age quicker. It's no coincidence that people who practice yoga over many years often look younger than their actual age.

Chronically tight muscles also leads to poor posture: our shoulders slump forward and our backs become rounded. This directly affects the functioning of the organs as blood flow is constricted. Bad posture also makes you look older and weaker and affects your mood in a negative way. Tightness in the hip, pelvis and hamstrings can also lead to backache later on in life. The practice of full-body stretching is a large subject and too much to cover in this book, however, most of the exercises in this section will concentrate on the back muscles, hamstrings and hips as these tend to be the tightest on most people.

It is better to carry out stretching on warm muscles hence the need for the warm up exercises before. You can also start with some light cardio exercises for ten to twenty minutes to warm up the muscles. There are three main stretches we will cover – the forward bend, the wide leg forward bend and the intestinal stretch.

Tina's Testimony

"I had a huge collection of workout videos dating back to the 90's. My bookshelves were filled with them. I also had every single piece of exercise equipment ever sold on the TV or in magazines - the abtronic, the 6-pack pumping chord band, the super trim-o-master. But nothing ever worked. I was always a size 12 and just couldn't get rid of that stubborn fat around my belly and my upper arms (my chicken wings). Doctors and gym instructors would just tell me that it was because of my genes, but I always felt that was just a 'cop-out' explanation. I knew I just wasn't doing the right exercise routine.

When I started the Zombie Plan, I really didn't expect it to work. I simply went through the motions. Surprisingly I found the 'human hunting' exercises quite exciting and I looked more and more forward to doing them in my workout. I didn't even think of them as a workout anymore and started training every day. But the real turning point came when I discovered that my dresses no longer fit me anymore. They were all too big and I needed to buy some new dresses - not once, but three more times as I lost more weight. Amazingly I'm now a size 8 and I feel great!"

Tina Wilkins, fitness buff

Forward bend

This exercise stretches the hamstrings, lower back and tendons behind the knees. As we get older, these muscles tighten and become shorter, making our legs weaker. This also contributes to bad posture, which constricts our organs making them less efficient. We become tired more easily and are more susceptible to various health complaints.

-    Sit on the floor with your spine erect and your legs close together.

-    Reach your arms above your head and then bending from the hip, reach forward for your feet.

-    Try to hold onto your two big toes, sides of feet or the backs of your knees. Then gently pull yourself forward.

-    Start to take some deep breaths and relax in the pose whilst always reaching forward.

-    Hold for one to three minutes and relax.

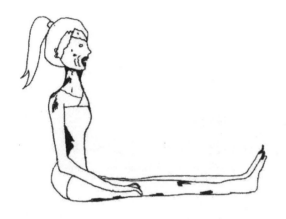

Sitting forward bend

Wide leg forward bend pose

This is a variation of the forward bend pose, which stretches the inner parts of the leg more.

- Sit on the floor with legs stretched in front of you and your spine erect.

- Open your legs as wide as they can go.

- Breathe in and reach your arms to the sky. As you breathe out, reach forward and touch the floor in front of you.

- Keep reaching your arms in front of your body. Over time, you will be able to touch your chest on the floor.

- Hold for one minute and release. If you want to vary the stretch, you can alternatively try to touch your left foot with your hands for thirty seconds and then your right foot to stretch the sides of the body.

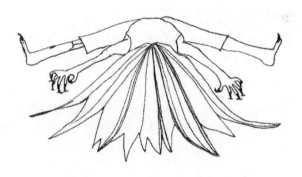

Wide leg forward bend pose

Intestinal stretch

This stretch is said to be able to cure diseases of the intestines. Some zombies will lie in this pose after eating a heavy meal to encourage digestion. It stretches the whole of the front part of body – the abdomen, intestines and stomach area.

- Kneel down on the floor. Fold your legs underneath your thigh and sit on your buttocks. You want to open your legs a little and place your bottom on the floor between your legs.

- Using your arms to support yourself, carefully lower yourself backwards and lie down.

- Reach your arms over your head and rest them on the ground over your head.

- Hold for thirty seconds to a minute. When getting out of the pose, carefully lift yourself back up using your arms.

You may want to rest in 'child's pose' (rest your torso forward over your knees) to relax your lower back after this pose.

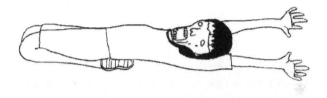

Intestinal Stretch

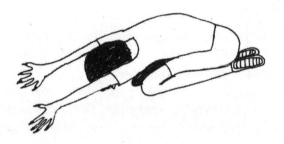

Child's Pose

Yoga

Yoga is an amazing system comprising of breathing, meditation, diet, philosophy and physical exercise (asanas), which can completely transform your mind and body.

Many people mistakenly think that only very flexible people can do yoga and may avoid trying it out. It's true that yoga classes do attract a lot of dancers and ex-gymnasts who already are incredibly flexible. However, yoga is a personal practice. Classes offer you the chance to break the mental conditioning of always trying to compare yourself to others. We are all different and have different bodies, which are always changing from one year to the next. Yoga is about getting in touch with your own body so that you can become aware of your own limitations and how you can push them.

Regular practice of yoga exercises can improve circulation, digestion, the immune system and posture. The subject of yoga is too large to include in this book, however we advise you to incorporate two or three yoga sessions into your weekly routine. If you are new to yoga, it is a good idea to go to a local class and get instruction from a teacher until you are confident to do the poses by yourself. Local classes are also a good source of high quality human meat for zombies. Alternatively, you can follow the exercises on a good yoga DVD.

Yoga in Bali

Strength building

Earlier we talked about the negative effects of stress on the body. One method to reduce stress and counteract the fight or flight response is to do vigorous exercise for five to ten minutes to work up a sweat. This metabolizes the excess stress hormones that will be circulating in the blood. The exercises in this section - the push ups, pull ups and squats are ideal for this purpose. These mini-sessions can easily fit into the day. It's quite easy to drop and do twenty or thirty push ups throughout the day. If you did five sets of twenty, you would have quite comfortably completed a hundred reps by the day's end – a great accomplishment, which can make us feel more positive due to the release of endorphins (good-mood chemicals).

The Zombie Plan 'strength building' exercises are not the same as bulking up. Some women avoid strength building exercises as they fear that they will put on too much muscle and look bulky. Bulking up is a different process, which is mostly followed by bodybuilders. In this case, bodybuilders will typically lift very heavy weights for a low number of repetitions and very few sets. They will also need to have rest days in between workouts as their muscles will be exhausted and need to recover.

The Zombie Exercise Plan differs in that it focuses on medium-weight exercises with more repetitions and sets. The idea is not to tire the body out too much that it needs a rest day to recover. Doing so can be detrimental. If you are too tired the day after working out, you may not be able to defend yourself against a zombie attack. What use are those big muscles then?

If we do a lot of repetitions of these exercises and more sets, the muscles will become more toned with greater definition and have more strength and resistance. These exercises can be done every day if desired.

Bob's Testimony

"My personal trainer always told me to "Feel the burn! Feel the burn!" I'd be at the gym three times a week. I'd do heavy lifting for my arms on Monday, my legs on Wednesday and my arms again on Friday. In between, I'd eat rump steak and drink protein shakes. I had size 18" biceps. I felt like superman on steroids.

But I always needed those rest days. After a day of heavy lifting, I felt as weak as a baby. Doing simple things like walking or opening the fridge door was painful. And then on one of those days, the zombies burst into my house.

It was just a group of elementary school zombie kids, but I couldn't hold them off. As they munched on my biceps I kept thinking, perhaps I should have tried a different training plan".

Bob Green, deceased

Strength building exercises

Push ups

The simple push up is a classic strength builder which works your arms, chest and upper body. You don't need any fancy equipment. It's just you and your body. As your strength increases, you can increase the number of repetitions and sets you do.

- Lie on the floor face down.

- Place your hands shoulder-width apart and extend your arms. Keep your body lifted and straight. This is the starting position.

- Lower yourself to the floor touching your chest to the ground, hold and then push yourself up again. This is one repetition.

- Repeat ten to twenty more times for one set and then rest. Aim to do five sets.

Some famous athletes and strongmen such as Herschel Walker and Charles Bronson have built powerful physiques using the simple push up as a primary exercise.

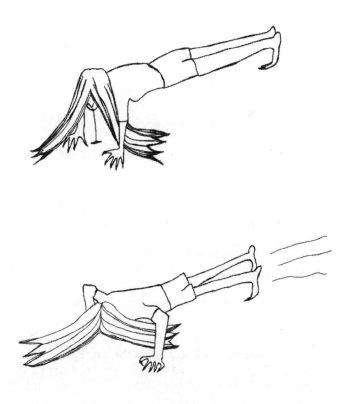

The classic push up

Pull ups

These are considered one of the ultimate bodyweight exercises as it requires you to lift almost 100% of your own weight. Unsurprisingly, they can be very hard for a beginner and a true test of determination. There are two types – the 'pull up', where your palms are facing away from you and the 'chin up', where your palms face towards you. The pull up builds grappling strength – an essential ability needed for zombies who regularly have to grapple humans of various sizes and strength.

-    Hold on to a bar or tree branch and let your body hang.

-    Using the strength of your arms, pull your body up so your chin goes higher than the bar.

-    Gently lower back to the starting position. That is one repetition.

-    Aim to do ten repetitions. Do pull ups throughout the day until you are able to complete thirty.

Important – don't cheat the exercise!

Some people keep their arms bent and biceps contracted when they lower themselves to make it easier. To get the benefits of this exercise, you should have your arms extended at the end of the rep. It may be harder, but it will be worth it.

Pull ups are a real test of strength

Leg raises

This exercise strengthens the lower abdomen, helping with posture and digestion.

- Lie on your back with arms by your side.

- Raise your legs off the ground together. Keep them straight.

- Lower your feet slowly back to the ground.

- Repeat twenty more times. Try to do five sets.

Often when people train their abdominals they will focus on doing sit-ups, especially if they want to build a 'six-pack'. The sit-up exercises are also recommended exercises.   However the leg raises are favoured because they work more on the lower abdominal muscles, which can become quite flaccid on many people.

The lower abdominal muscles have an important role in holding the torso upright. Regular leg raises can make you feel stronger in the lower belly and help maintain good upright posture.

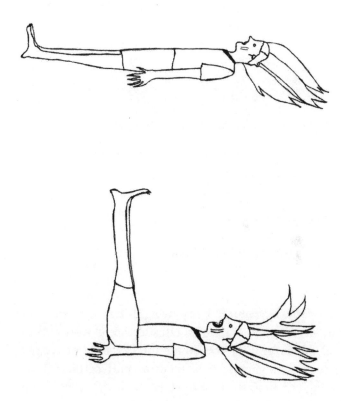

Leg raises helps build abdominal strength

Leg squats

The legs are the foundation of the body. They must support us in all our activities. As we get older, our legs get weaker and our power diminishes. The free-weight squat tones and strengthens our legs. It is also possible to increase the intensity of this exercise by holding onto other body-weights like a human torso while you perform the exercise.

- Stand with feet shoulder-width apart.

- Bend your knees and lower your body till your thighs are parallel with the floor.

- Raise yourself up to the starting position. This is one repetition.

- Do a set of fifty repetitions.

Some famous natural body weight trainers, such as Charles Atlas and the Indian wrestler Gama were able to build powerful thighs by doing hundreds of free weight leg squats or variations of them as part of their daily training. At first, it's best to start off slowly. Aim to do fifty a day and gradually increase by five more each day. Within weeks you could be doing hundreds.

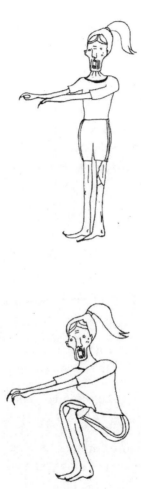

Leg squats tone your butt

Bridge pose

This is a yogic pose which is also used as part of gymnastic training to condition the body. It opens the chest encouraging circulation to the heart and lungs. It can open up emotional blocks which are often held in the chest or abdomen. The thymus and lymph nodes (part of the immune system) are stimulated and the muscles of the back are strengthened making you stand taller and straighter.

- Lie on your back. Bend your legs and lay your feet on the ground as close to your bottom as possible. Bend your elbows and place your hands by the side of your head.

- Lift your body into the air by pushing into your feet and hands.

- Try to straighten your arms and legs by pushing further into the stretch. Don't strain.

- Hold for thirty seconds and gently lower to the ground.

- Repeat five more times. As you get stronger, increase the amount of time you hold the pose.

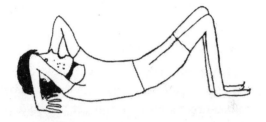

The bridge

Handstand

The handstand is another intense exercise requiring you to lift almost 100% of your bodyweight. The forearms are especially worked out in the handstand. Zombies need strong forearms to rip flesh off bone and to pull out internal organs so this exercise is ideal.

For a beginner, you may not have the strength to hold your body up without support, so it is acceptable to use a wall to balance against. As you get more adept at this exercise, you may want to gently try moving your feet away from the wall until you can balance just by yourself.

- Facing a wall, place your hands on the ground close to the wall about shoulder-width apart.

- Use one leg to propel yourself and flip your legs up over your body resting them on the wall. Keep your arms strong or you will fall!

- Hold for thirty seconds and gently bring your feet back down one at a time.

- Repeat three more times. As you get stronger, you can aim to hold the pose for longer.

Handstands build strong forearms for ripping off flesh

Stamina building exercises

You may have tailored suits, expensive jewellery, expensive aftershave or perfume. You may be toned and strong, but if you have poor stamina and are easily winded when being chased, you will only make a good meal for a zombie. As zombies have impaired brain function, they are not able to operate motor vehicles or use weapons like spears or guns. Zombies must hunt for their food similar to a tiger or lion. They must chase and rip their prey into bits. It is essential for zombies to have good stamina therefore they train their lungs and legs every day with the exercises in this chapter. If humans follow these exercises they also will improve their stamina.

The best thing about most stamina exercises is that they are relatively inexpensive. It's worth bearing in mind that zombies train 'old school'. They often train outside in the local neighbourhood and not in fancy gyms.

For best results, it is ideal to do a minimum of twenty minutes cardio every day, although if you can't manage this - three to four times a week will give you benefits. Before starting, you should do a gentle warm up and stretch for a few minutes. Here are some of the best kinds of cardiovascular exercises to get you as fit as a zombie:

Jogging

Jogging is the most versatile of exercises. All you need are a pair of running shoes, but even these aren't necessary as many zombies opt to run in regular shoes or even barefoot.   You don't need a running machine as you can customize the terrain to your workout. For example, if you want a steady jog, you can run along the road. If you want a more intense exercise, you can run up and down stairwells in city tower-blocks. Or if you want the fresh air of nature, you can jog along the beach or cross country. It is ideal to train in different terrains for zombies as it is often necessary to chase humans in many different places.

Jogging increases your lung capacity, which provides more oxygen to the body organs. Jogging speeds up the heart rate and strengthens the heart muscle. Other benefits are increased metabolism and a stronger immune system. The best time to run is in the morning especially first thing after you wake up. But don't jog on a full stomach. It is best to eat breakfast after jogging, although some zombies will plop a few eyes in a glass for a high protein kick before hitting the road.

Jogging is a practical exercise for zombies as they spend a lot of time chasing humans for nourishment. Jogging can also be very stress relieving. During distance running, if you have any problems in life, long distance jogging gives you the chance to be alone with only your thoughts. A chance to un-clutter your mind and release some stress.

Jogging can also be a fun social activity. If you join local jogging groups, you can enjoy the camaraderie of being with like-minded people.

Jogging is a fun social activity

Swimming

Swimming is a great exercise which works every muscle of your body. It tones your physique and strengthens your heart and lungs. It improves flexibility and co-ordination. Zombies love swimming because it is a low impact exercise. Many zombies have joint and muscular problems caused by wounds and the general wear and tear associated with death such as rigor mortis. Swimming puts 90% less stress on the joints: the knees, ankles and hips then other sports and is excellent for rehabilitation. Swimming requires taking deep co-ordinated breaths and is great for strengthening our lungs. If you adopt a habit of swimming, your posture can also improve.

There are four main strokes used in recreational swimming: the front crawl, breaststroke, backstroke and the more challenging butterfly. Even untrained swimmers can start with the doggie paddle, where they use their arms and legs and mimic the movement of a dog. The beauty of swimming is that even a zombie with a missing limb or injured body part can still swim by adapting their strokes. This style of swimming is generally known as the 'zombie-stroke'.

Water aerobics is a popular exercise in many leisure centers. This is where humans perform gentle aerobic classes to music using the resistance of water to provide a stronger workout. Zombies have a superior alternative to this called the 'zombie-wade'. As its name suggests, this is the process of wading or walking in the water. Some zombies will walk up to a mile at the bottom of a river or lake as part of their training, especially to get to an island full of human survivors. This is not recommended for humans.

Here is a sample swimming program for a beginner:

- Swim for five lengths of breast stroke. Then rest for five minutes.

- Swim for five lengths of crawl. Then rest for five minutes.

- Do five lengths of back stroke. Then rest for five minutes.

- Finish with five lengths of breaststroke.

Hint:

The correct swimming equipment can help you get the most out of swimming. A good quality pair of goggles are useful especially if you are hunting for humans underwater. Leisure center changing rooms are also a great place to find unsuspecting humans to hunt and eat. Don't forget to bring your own shower gel and shampoo to wash out all that chlorine and blood.

Swimming stretches all the muscles of the body

Cycling

Cycling is a cheaper, less polluting means of getting around and provides you with a great workout. Cycling tones and strengthens the leg muscles and builds stamina. Cycling also improves co-ordination and balance, which is especially beneficial to zombies who have terrible co-ordination problems. Zombies may occasionally cycle when hunting, particularly if their prey is especially fast. For a beginner, it is beneficial to start by going cycling once or twice a week. Decide on a distance and gradually increase it as you get more accustomed to cycling.

Investing in a good bicycle is advisable, especially if you are going to hunt for humans. You may be familiar with the so-called 'grandmother bike'. This common bicycle is basic in design and has a basket on the front. It can be useful if you want to carry your groceries or a human head back home. However they are quite slow and also somewhat 'uncool'. I would recommend a stylish off-road mountain bike. If you want to carry body parts to sustain you, you can always carry them in a backpack.

In some countries it is a legal requirement that you wear a helmet. Helmets can protect your head if you fall off your bike. Zombies have limited brain function so it's often a good idea for them to wear helmets to protect what little brain matter they have left.

Cycling helps with balance and co-ordination

Skipping

Zombies are lean, fit, fighting creatures. But they did not invent the exercises in this book. It is no secret that skipping is a favoured exercise of boxers and is one of the methods they use to reach the peak of fitness. All you need are a pair of running shoes, a rope and space. A stopwatch can help you keep time. If you don't have a rope, you can use some small intestine. Just adjust the length to suit you.

Jogging strengthens the muscles and increases the bone density especially in the back, hips and legs. In some ways, skipping is better than jogging. One of the problems with jogging is that it can put a lot of stress on the knees especially when jogging on concrete. Joggers can suffer from shin-splints if they run too much on hard surfaces. In skipping, there is less stress on the knee as the impact of jumping is absorbed by the balls of the feet rather than the heels. Did you know that ten minutes of skipping is the equivalent of running an eight minute mile?

There are many variations of skipping, but the two most common are the 'basic' and 'alternate' jumps. In the basic jump, the feet are a little apart and both feet jump together over the rope. In the alternate jump, you alternate your feet, jumping with your left foot, then right and then left and so on. This method enables you to skip faster.

Skipping warms up and loosens stiff joints

Hill walking

When you get bored of jogging and swimming, it is your mind's way of telling you to add variety to your exercise program. This is where hill walking provides you with a completely different kind of workout. Hill walking challenges your heart, lungs and legs. All you need is to find a hill or small mountain and walk for a period of time. By walking uphill, you will also be working a completely different set of muscles in your leg – the gluteals, calves and hamstrings. The benefits of hill walking are that it is free and also gives you the chance to get some fresh air and to reconnect with nature. You'll be amazed at the beautiful scenery. Occasionally zombies will walk up hills and be surprised to find small colonies of humans surviving. The day after walking up a hill, be prepared to have aching legs - the good kind of ache.

It's a good idea to invest in the right clothing if you're going to walk up hills or mountains. Good walking shoes, a hat to shield you from the sun, a rain jacket and backpack to carry some flesh in are essential items. Also carry a light flask in which you can bring some blood to drink to prevent you from becoming dehydrated.

Hill walking reconnects you with nature

The quiet-down: yin and yang

In traditional Chinese medicine, there is the concept of yin and yang. Yin and yang are polar opposites, present in everything in the Universe. Yang is considered light, the sun, that which is seen and the expansion of energy. Yin reflects the dark, the moon, the hidden and the conservation of energy. Yin and yang reflects balance.

In human fitness, physical activity and exercise is yang in nature, whereas resting and recuperating is yin. If we do too much exercise and no rest (too much yang) our bodies become exhausted and collapse. If we do no exercise at all (too much yin), our bodies become very weak and sick. If the balance between yin and yang is correct, our bodies will be healthy. After doing all these physical exercises in this book, we need to replenish our yin energy – our internal strength. This is why the sitting and breathing exercises are very important.

The balance of yin and yang is very important to a zombie. They will sit quietly meditating in dark alleys or in the shade (yin) and wait for humans.   When a human appears, they will chase after it and violently eat its flesh (yang activity). The meat is protein (a yang food), but they eat it raw (yin). After eating, they will sleep and digest their meal (yin activity).

Sitting

After challenging your body with exercise, it is important to sit in quiet reflection and allow these changes to settle in your body. Sitting exercises can be used at any time in the day when you want to re-energize and focus your mind. There are two sitting postures: the lotus and seiza.

Seiza

Seiza translates as 'correct sitting' in Japanese. The advantage of this pose is that it's easy to get up from the floor if you suddenly see a human running past. You simply lift up one leg first and stand up.

Kneel down, fold your legs under your thigh and sit on your buttocks. You may wish to touch your toes together for extra comfort. Hold your spine erect and place your hands on your lap.

You can practice deep breathing or meditate as you sit quietly waiting for humans to appear.   At the beginning, your feet may get some pins and needles. To relieve this, it may be necessary to move them around from time to time.

Seiza

Lotus

The lotus is a deeper meditative pose than the seiza. Cross your legs and keep your spine erect. If you are very flexible you can fold your legs on top of each other. If you are not that flexible, you can do a half-lotus, where you tuck just the one leg over the other.

Close your eyes and let the thoughts come and go without any concern. As zombies have impaired brain function, doing this is easy for them. The benefits of this kind of meditation is that it lowers the heart beat, calms the body and puts the body in a state of relaxation, which benefits the immune system. It also gently opens up the hips.

Lotus

Humans and zombies alike have a lot of stresses in life to deal with. Humans are stressed with bills, jobs, relationships and with becoming extinct. Some zombies are stressed with the implications of a declining human population and the challenge of finding their next meal. If our days are full of stress, we take this stress to sleep with us. Our minds are always looking for solutions to our problems and will try to deal with this during our sleep, resulting in nightmares and restlessness. By going into a meditative state, we allow our subconscious mind to work on the issue during the day. After meditation, we often feel more refreshed and our minds more alert.

Breathing

As we talked earlier, the lack of physical exercise and fresh air among many humans has led to shallow breathing causing rounded shoulders and sunken chests. The average human does not breathe to the full capacity of their lungs. The lungs are designed to bring oxygen into the body to be used in energy production and to remove waste products like carbon dioxide. The lungs have three sections - a top, middle and bottom section. However the majority of humans will often only breathe into the top two sections leaving stale air in the bottom. By deep breathing we can recycle all the air in the lungs. Regular deep breathing will also increase the size of the chest gradually as all the rib muscles are gently stretched. It is also believed that some diseases can be healed with regular deep breathing.

The best way to practice deep breathing is in the seiza or lotus sitting poses, although you can practice it in any position and at any time. It is best to keep the spine straight to allow more space for your chest to open up.

Breathe in slowly through your nose and keep your mouth closed. Breathe the air deeply into your lower abdomen. You should see your belly expand – not your chest. If your chest expands, then it means you are probably not breathing deep enough. Hold the breath for a short moment and then slowly breathe out. Your belly will slowly become smaller.

This is a simple breathing exercise, but there are more variations. Aim to breathe for about ten minutes at first and gradually increase the length of time.

You can also practice deep breathing at any time when you get stressed. When we are stressed, the fight or flight mechanism kicks in and our breathing rate increases and becomes shallower. By deep breathing we counteract this signal, which enables us to think more rationally and react to the stressful situation more intelligently. For example, if we are confronted by a crazed blood-thirsty zombie, our initial reaction is to run away in a panic. Unfortunately, if we are not careful we may run straight into a pack of zombies around the corner. If we take a few deep breaths and evaluate the situation, we may notice a weakness in the zombie or find a weapon close-by, with which we can use to overcome it with. Breathing is a technique used by martial artists to retain composure whilst fighting.

Sheila's Testimony

"I thought that I was happily married. My husband was a successful stockbroker. We had a huge house and went on tropical holidays every year. However, despite our wealth, I felt deeply unsatisfied. I was bored with seeing the same friends (wives of other stockbrokers) and our endless shopping trips. I wanted to have my own life – not just be the good wife. I wanted to feel alive. I started overeating and drinking whisky in the day. Fortunately an old university friend pushed me to try the Zombie Plan.

At first the exercises really helped build my self confidence. I lost weight and became stronger, but I still had trouble eating raw meat. I just couldn't get used to it. I realize now, that this was my old negative thought-pattern holding me back. The turning point came one day when my husband told me he was leaving me for his secretary. He actually accused me of being boring. Something snapped inside of me.

I ate my husband and then I devoured his secretary and I felt so good afterwards. To celebrate, I couldn't resist a glass of wine to wash them down. I know it's not in the rules, but I think a little cheat now and again is ok. I'm now so much thinner. I feel more positive and for the first time I felt able to follow my own life path. Soon after I finally decided to start my own business. All thanks to the Zombie Plan".

Sheila Jesseton-Winehurst, Interior Designer

Chapter 5

The Zombie Diet

Why do zombies eat humans?

Why do zombies prefer to eat humans over other mammals like birds or dogs? Actually zombies will eat all meats that are available, but humans are the favoured choice for several reasons.

Prior to the appearance of zombies, humans sat at the top of the food chain. Humans had no natural predators and could eat pretty much everything they wanted. For example, a carrot would be eaten by a rabbit, which is eaten by a snake, which can then be eaten by a human. Grass is eaten by an earthworm, which is eaten by a bird, which can then be eaten by a human. This means that humans, by virtue of sitting at the top of the food chain can consume nutrients not just from one animal, but from several sources all in one meal. Indeed the human is a storehouse of valuable nutrients and this is the reason why the human is the zombie's favoured meal.

Another reason is down to the easy availability of humans. Due to the increasing birth-rate in the first quarter of the 21st century and in spite of various attempts to cull their own population by drugs, poverty and war - there were approximately seven billion humans worldwide. Humans naturally came to be the primary source of livestock for zombies. Humans also tended to congregate and be concentrated in small economic zones otherwise known as cities, where they would live in small box-like rooms called apartment complexes. These living conditions made it easy to hunt humans in large numbers.

In the rest of this chapter, we will look at the nutrients that are needed by the body and the best sources to find these foods.

Protein

When water is removed from the body, 75 percent of your weight is protein. Protein is found in muscle, bone, skin, hair and virtually every other body part or tissue. It is an essential nutrient for the human body.   Proteins are broken down in the body into amino acids, which are one of the building blocks of body tissue. They can also be used as a source of energy.

Amino acids can be classified into 'essential' and 'non-essential' amino acids. Essential amino acids cannot be made by the body and must be supplied by food.

Non-essential amino acids can be made in the body. If a food contains enough essential amino acids, it is called a complete protein. If not, it is called an incomplete protein. For zombies and humans it is important to consume enough 'complete' proteins. Fortunately, the human body is made up of complete proteins.

Eating protein daily is important because the body doesn't store amino acids, as it does fats or carbohydrates. It needs a daily supply of amino acids to make new protein. It is also important for zombies to consume enough protein as a lack can cause a loss of muscle mass, decreased immunity and a weak heart. Good sources of complete proteins are human muscles, pets, horses and zoo animals.

Protein contains the B vitamins (niacin, thiamin, riboflavin and B6), vitamin E, iron, zinc, and magnesium. Protein functions as building blocks for the bones, muscles, cartilage, skin and blood. The best amount for a human adult to eat is fifty to one hundred grams a day, but when you are following the Zombie Plan, you need a lot more protein than this. To measure an adequate serving of protein in a meal, you can follow the 'palm rule':

A simple way to measure is - three times each day you should consume about the amount of protein you are able to rip off and hold in the palms of both your hands. This should be about the size of a human head.

Fat

Though it may sound like a contradiction, eating fat can help with losing weight, but it has to be the right kind of fat. Eating fat causes the release of leptin: a hormone that sends signals to the brain that the body is full. This signal naturally stops us from over-eating excess calories which is the main cause of weight-gain. So you see that fat can keep us physically full and psychologically satisfied. Mono and polyunsaturated fats are the healthiest and the two most beneficial kinds of polyunsaturated fats are omega 3 and omega 6 fatty acids. These are usually found in vegetables and oily fish (and humans who eat these foods a lot). Omega 3 improves elasticity and the muscle tone of the skin, making you appear youthful. Saturated fats are found in butter or lard (and people who eat a lot of fried foods). They also have some benefits, although should be eaten in moderation.

The best source of fat is the human brain. It is made up of about 60% fat, which comes from the myelin. The hardest aspect of eating the brain is that it can be hard to get to it due to the skull which acts as a strong protective shield for the brain. In order to access the brain, a blunt item may be required. However once through the skull, the brain itself does not have any pain receptors so while you eat, your prey will not be troublesomely screaming or moving in agony which can be quite distracting for a zombie trying to enjoy his meal.

Warning

Saturated fats contain high levels of cholesterol and fatty substances that can lead to arteriosclerosis and heart disease. Saturated fats are at high levels in humans who consume large amounts of butter, lard, margarine and junk foods.

You've probably noticed that the average zombie tends to be slim and athletic. Even though zombies will often eat humans with a lot of saturated fat, they are able to burn off this excess by being more active: by hunting, walking and grappling with humans.

Generally, it is easier for a zombie to eat a human with a large amount of saturated fat as they will tend to be slower and heavier and more prone to tiredness and breathlessness when being chased. Unsurprisingly, when the first zombie outbreak occurred, it was the most overweight humans that were the first to be eaten.

Nonetheless, zombies still have to be careful as these high levels of saturated fats can cause zombies to be sluggish, irritable and also overweight themselves. Humans with a lot of saturated fat should be eaten in moderation. A few mouthfuls of the most lean muscle areas like the feet should suffice.

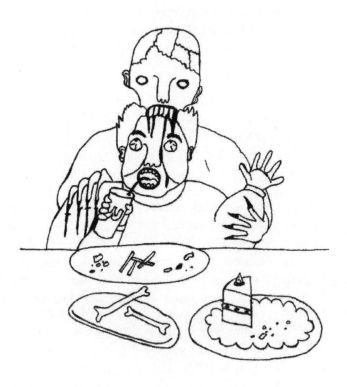

Be wary of eating too much saturated fat

Carbohydrates

For most humans, carbohydrates provide their main source of energy. Carbohydrates are made of sugars which are broken down into fuel. 'Simple' carbohydrates, such as candies or white bread break down quickly in the body causing the blood sugar levels to increase rapidly. On the other hand, 'complex' carbohydrates such as wholegrain and fibrous vegetables break down steadily and slowly providing longer lasting energy.

Carbohydrates are the fuel of the brain because the brain requires glucose or sugar to function. However, carbohydrates are not an essential nutrient as humans can create glucose from burning proteins (amino acids) and fats to feed the brain.

There are some health issues with eating an excess of carbohydrates. Consuming carbohydrates that raise your blood sugar levels too quickly (like cake and white bread) can over time cause you to develop diabetes. This is an increasing problem in affluent countries as the consumption of refined white flour and processed foods is higher. These foods are typically stripped of good nutrients, vitamins and minerals. As the body is short of these needed nutrients, many people still feel hungry and crave foods. There is a tendency to eat more, which is stored as fat. This can lead to obesity especially excess weight around the stomach area, thighs and buttocks. There is also a greater risk of heart disease, stroke and high blood pressure.

Complex carbohydrates like vegetables and wholegrain foods do have health benefits for humans. Fortunately for zombies, the vast majority of humans eat inferior simple carbohydrates instead, causing a great many of them to be overweight and sick. This makes it easier to catch and eat them.

The Zombie Plan Diet is a natural low carbohydrate diet. One of the advantages that the zombie has: is that due to his impaired brain function there is a smaller requirement for glucose for the brain. The smaller amounts needed to fuel the zombie brain can easily be made from protein hence they don't need to eat carbohydrates. As zombies don't eat carbohydrates, they put on less weight making them more slim and athletic.

Fibre

Fibre is a part of plant food that cannot be digested by humans. There are two types of fibre: soluble and insoluble fibre. Soluble fibre dissolves in water and forms a gel-like substance in the intestines. Soluble fibre comes from oats, legumes, apples and bananas. Insoluble fibre does not dissolve in water. It acts as a form of roughage which helps the movement of food through the digestive tract. It can be found in wholewheat, bran, nuts and seeds. Fibre is believed to be beneficial to humans because it prevents constipation by making the stool bulky and soft. It also lowers blood cholesterol, reduces the risk of colon cancer, heart disease and digestive diseases like diverticulitis. It improves blood sugar levels and helps reduce overeating as it makes people feel fuller.

Despite these benefits, fibre is not an essential nutrient for humans. A human will not die if they don't eat it, and there are cultures in the world that eat almost no fibre such as the Inuit of Alaska and the African Masai.

Fibre is not necessary for zombie nutrition. Zombies avoid fibre because it can lead to decreased nutrient and mineral absorption. This is due to the gel-like substance from soluble fibre that forms in the intestines. This gel prevents digestive enzymes from getting to the food, which then gets pushed out of the body. Dietary fibres can also hinder the absorption of minerals especially calcium, magnesium, sodium and potassium. For zombies that have a greater need for nutrients, this loss is detrimental. And even though fibre has the benefit of preventing constipation, zombies deal with this problem by consuming plenty of water from human flesh and encouraging peristalsis of their intestines by regularly exercising and hunting.

Vitamins & Minerals

Vitamins are substances made by plants or animals. Minerals are elements from the earth, soil and water, which are absorbed by plants. Vitamins and minerals are needed by the body to grow and to maintain your health. Deficiencies in some minerals or vitamins can cause various health problems. Despite their importance, you will never see zombies taking vitamin or mineral supplements. This is because they can get everything they need from human meat.

Vitamin C

Vitamin C or ascorbic acid is important for the immune system and producing connective tissue. A good dose of vitamin C protects the body from infection, maintains healthy bones and teeth as well as promotes wound healing. It is an essential nutrient for zombies as they often have impaired immune systems and open wounds and also require very strong teeth in order to tear human flesh off bones. Good sources of vitamin C can be found in the human liver, lungs and cartilage (the white crunchy substance between the bones and in the ears).

Vitamin A

Vitamin A is essential for maintaining healthy bones and teeth. It is needed to make dentin – the hard layer of material within teeth. Vitamin A helps replace worn out tissue.

Again, this is an essential nutrient for the health of zombie's teeth. The human liver is a good source of vitamin A.

Vitamin D

Vitamin D can be synthesised in the human body from exposure to sunlight. It is needed to help the intestines to absorb nutrients: especially calcium and phosphorus, which ensures strong bones. It is an especially important nutrient for zombies. Vitamin D also reduces muscle spasms which reduces pain. Good sources are human brain, flesh and skin.

B complex vitamins

This is a family of vitamins. B vitamins help in regulating the nervous system, reducing depression, stress and brain shrinkage. They also help maintain a strong digestive system. Deficiencies in B vitamins can cause illnesses like anaemia, fatigue, weakness and weight loss. The B complex vitamins are very important to zombies as a lack in this vitamin can severely impact on a zombie's performance. Zombies already have damaged brains, so they need to preserve what little brain function they have left. It is important for zombies to eat three to four times the recommended daily allowance of B vitamins for excellent health. Good sources of B vitamins are the human liver, brain, stomach and intestines. The tongue also contains a high amount of vitamin B12.

Calcium

For strong bones and teeth, calcium is essential. Humans and zombies alike need strong bones to support their bodies through day to day living. Zombies in particular need strong teeth to bite the meat from human bones and chew on it. However we also need vitamin D in order to absorb calcium. The best source of vitamin D can be created in the body when it is exposed to sunlight. So hunting for humans in daylight, especially during the summer is really important to zombies, not to mention the great tan they can get.

Human bones are full of calcium. Chewing and sucking on human finger bones is one way to get some of this mineral. Calcium is abundant in dairy products, milk, cheese and yoghurt and also bony oily fish like salmon and sardines. Another strategy would be to consume humans who eat a lot of these foods: in particular dairy farmers and fishermen.

Iron

Zombies don't drink coke, soda, tea, coffee, beer, spirits or even protein shakes. A zombie's favourite drink is blood. Blood contains iron which is needed to make haemoglobin in the blood cells and which transports oxygen around the body and to the brain. Higher iron levels means more haemoglobin and more oxygen can be transported throughout the body making the body more energetic. Blood contains around 40 - 50% of the iron in the human body. It is the perfect energy drink and may be the secret to the zombie's high energy levels, as one marathon client said:

Joe's Testimony

"I used to be a marathon runner doing maybe three or four races a year, so I'm no stranger to long distance running and training for endurance. I was not concerned when this zombie started running after me. I thought I could easily outrun him. After ten miles, he was still with me growling and snapping away. I thought he surely couldn't last much longer now, but twenty-five miles later he was still there, growling away looking as fresh as when we first started, while I was sweating and panting and almost ready to collapse. Finally he caught me. I realised then, that the zombie was much fitter than I was".

Joe Biles, deceased

The best source of iron is blood. Arteries on the neck and wrist can provide a flow of blood if bitten into. Alternatively, pull out and suck on the heart. The liver is also a good source of iron. Remember it is on the right side of the body. If you rip out an organ from the left side, chances are, you may pull out the spleen or pancreas by mistake. Check the recipes section for a good liver sushi.

Chapter 6

Zombie Plan: The rules

By this point, it is necessary to clarify some aspects of the Zombie Exercise and Diet Plan.

First, you do not need to be a zombie to follow this program. It isn't necessary to go out and get infected by a zombie. This diet is designed for humans who want to enjoy the same levels of strength and fitness as the zombie. It goes without saying, that most zombies already know and practice the principles in this book, but even so, this book can also benefit zombies. It may show them some new exercises that they are not aware of and new diet ideas.

This book can also be useful for someone who has just been bitten and infected, and is in the process of turning into a zombie. You can use your last remaining hours as a human, reading this book and preparing yourself for when you 'turn'.

Secondly, in order to follow this diet, you will have to eat raw human flesh. This is a key point of the diet. I understand that a lot of humans have trouble with this concept: that it is morally wrong and disgusting, but as I have explained - human meat has so many nutritional benefits and is one of the reasons the zombie is so powerful. There is no compromise here.

On top of that, you must also hunt the humans yourself. You cannot sit back and eat the carcass of human remains killed several days ago by some other zombie. Nor can you only eat animal meat. One time, I had a female client who only ate her neighbour's dogs. Unsurprisingly, that client made little progress – she couldn't lose weight and suffered from constipation. I had to explain that the process of hunting and grappling with a human is also a 'power exercise' with the amazing ability to burn calories and increase strength. Fortunately, that person agreed to start hunting humans and leave the neighbour's pets alone. A few weeks later, I met her again. Even I was astounded at the transformation that had occurred in my client. Her musculature was toned. Her skin glowed with paleness and she had regular bowel movements.

Thirdly, although you are adopting the zombie diet and training techniques, you do not have to emanate the zombie. You can still shower and wear clean clothes. You can still work a regular job and you can still live in a house if you want to. However as you adopt the Zombie Plan, you may find yourself becoming less materialistic and want to start simplifying your life. You may see less meaning behind the pursuit of money, of eight-hour work-days, and the endless consumption of clothes, cars and accessories. Some of my clients even went so far as to quit their high-paying corporate jobs in the city and switch to the zombie lifestyle completely. Many of them found more fulfilment in wearing rags and wandering aimlessly around the streets cannibalising humans, then they ever did in their jobs. All this was made possible with the Zombie Plan.

The Zombie Plan can help with workplace stress

So just to recap: in the previous chapters you have read all the science behind the plan. Now here are the principles:

- 90% of your food should be from human meat. 10% can come from animals but be wary of choking on animal fur. Humans are generally cleaner than animals. Women especially tend to have a pleasant scent.

- Avoid carbs. No need to eat bread, pasta, rice or cakes. They are not necessary to make energy because glucose can be converted from protein. Carbohydrates make zombies fat.

- No fibre. No fruits or vegetables. Fruits and cruciferous vegetables like cabbage are often wind forming. It is quite hard to stalk and hunt humans stealthily, while suffering from gas.

- Don't overeat - Focus on two to three meals a day. Try having a big breakfast and a big dinner to help sleep. Have a very light lunch to avoid the post-afternoon slump. Some light snacking throughout the day is allowed on fingers, bones or eyes. Eat till 80% of your stomach is full and don't forget to chew your food.

- Eat freshly captured raw humans. Don't be picky about what part of the human to eat. Eat immediately for maximum absorption of nutrients and enzymes.

- Practice periodic or intermittent fasting. It helps clean out the system, enabling the body to run more efficiently. For two or three times a week, it can be beneficial to eat just one or two meals daily.

- Exercise every day for a minimum of thirty minutes. Alternate gentle exercises, such as walking and stretching with high intensity exercises like push-ups or sprinting (after humans).

Diet Plan

Below is a sample diet plan which you can adapt and modify to suit your own needs. You do not need to be a great cook. The recipes are very simple to prepare.

Breakfast:

3 slices of cerebellum layered over a lean piece of jogger's thigh with a juicy mouthful of aortic blood gravy.

In oriental dietary philosophy, the stomach is at the peak of its power between 7 and 9 am. For breakfast, it is good to eat a filling muscle-meal with some brain to last you throughout the day. The fats in the brain will balance your sugar levels and help you concentrate throughout the day.

Lunch:

Eyeball mousse, with earlobe sashimi and lung alveoli salad.

This Japanese inspired recipe is light and easy to digest. A light meal at lunch can help prevent the post afternoon slump that can come from eating heavy meals.

Dinner:

Artery soup starter, followed by liver a la tartare and rare rump steak.

It's a good idea to eat a heavier meal at dinner containing some carbohydrates (from the liver). These sugars help produce serotonin in the body – a mood chemical, which can help you have a good night's sleep. Select a good cut of meat from the gluteus maximus muscle. If it is a social occasion, it is a good idea to obtain an alcohol-fed-human. The liver from such a human can provide a nice lift to your guests.

Snacks:

Sliced skin, black pudding cubes (congealed blood), crunchy earlobes.

For those periods between meals when you want something to keep your energy levels steady but don't want to overeat.

There are many opportunities for you to express your creativity when preparing meals. Several Zombie Plan Diet eaters incorporate the use of blenders, food processors and juicers to make exciting smoothies and soups. Just remember to eat your food raw and as soon as possible to preserve all the vitamins and enzymes.

In the next chapter, we will look at some fabulous recipes in detail to inspire you.

Lunchbox Tips!

It's always a good idea to bring a lunchbox of titbits for those times when you are hungry and not able to find somebody to eat. They can also be great for kid's lunchboxes at school.

Try putting some crunchy toes and chewy eyelids with some minced spleen into your box. If you are creative, you can arrange the toes into a pattern. You'll find it a cheaper and more filling option than buying your food from the local cafe.

Chapter 7

Recipes

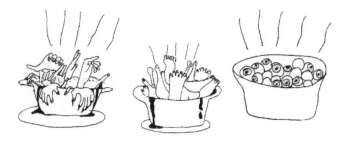

Hand and foot pot-au-feu

Eyeball soup

Human head

Liver sushi

Eyeball soup

A delightful light entree packed full of nutrients and flavour.

Serves 2

20 sets of human eyes

1 pint of human blood

400g of human skin

Pluck the eyes from the eye sockets. Marinade in the blood for twenty minutes in a large glass bowl. Shred the skin with a grater.

Place the eyeballs in a large serving dish.

Sprinkle the shredded skin flakes over the eyes.

Pour the left-over marinated blood into wine glasses and enjoy with the meal.

Liver sushi

Sushi is the ideal finger food. Remind your guests that they should pick it up and eat with their hands.

Serves 4

1/2 pound of human liver

20 fingers

Wasabi paste

Chop the fingers and arrange on plates.

Slice the liver with a very sharp knife.

Place a slice of liver on each finger and serve.

Add a little wasabi to flavour.

Hand and foot pot-au-feu

This classic French dish is modified for a discerning zombie palate.

Serves 6

10 pairs of arms and legs

A large vat of visceral fat

A pint of human sputum

Dijon mustard

Chop the arms and feet off the bodies.

Throw the limbs into the (unheated) vat of visceral fat and stir for twenty minutes with a thigh bone.

Put onto plates and pour a tablespoon of sputum over each serving.

Add dijon for flavour.

Chapter 8

Zombie Food Choices

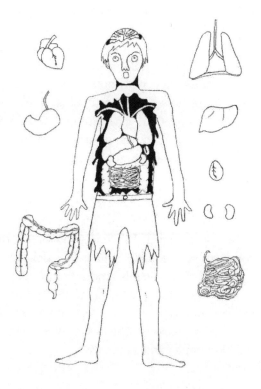

Zombie challenge! Can you match the offal to the names – brain, heart, lungs, liver, stomach, spleen, kidneys, large intestine and small intestine?

Blood

Blood is the ultimate power drink containing lots of iron. Many cultures around the world eat blood as food. Some uses are: as a form of blood sausage or black pudding, a thickener for sauces or a blood soup. Raw blood can also be consumed straight or added to other drinks and dishes. The Inuit people of the Arctic often drink seal blood. Afterwards they will look at the veins in their wrist and admire how they would expand and darken, becoming more fortified. The human body contains around five litres of blood made up of red blood cells, white blood cells, platelets and blood plasma.

Bone marrow

The bones may be hard, but once you break through them you can find a fatty gelatinous delicacy. Bone marrow contains a reasonable amount of protein and the great thing is that the fat is not saturated. Marrow also contains iron and calcium. The leg bones contain the largest amount of marrow. The best way to eat this food is to break them open and suck away.

Brain

Following various popular 1980's zombie movies, the zombie is often associated with being obsessed with eating brains. This is only partly true. The zombie enjoys eating all parts of the body. In fact, the brain is quite a difficult organ to get access to because it is protected by the skull. Nonetheless, zombies do enjoy eating brains. Human brains contain a large concentration of DHA - an important Omega-3 fatty acid. This is found in the myelin. It is also a very soft, easy digestible food and quite suitable for zombies with false teeth or the elderly. Use a blunt object to open up the skull and suck it out.

The prion controversy

A few words should be said about the subject of 'prions'. Opponents of the Zombie Diet often claim that eating brain is dangerous because abnormal infectious proteins called 'prions' are passed on when eating the brain. These prions 'eats' holes in the nervous system causing diseases such as mad-cow disease, chronic wasting disease and kuru. Opponents often refer to the cannibalistic 'Fore' people of Papua New Guinea as an example. The 'Fore' people regularly eat human brains and many suffer with the symptoms of kuru disease – trembling limbs and pathological bursts of manic laughter. To refute this, there are no accounts of zombies suffering from this disease to date. In fact, zombies actually get healthier when they eat brains. In all the time I've been teaching the Zombie Exercise and Diet Plan, none of my clients has ever suffered from this disease. I believe that this is just a bit of scaremongering.

Muscles

Muscles provide one of the best sources of protein and are abundant in the human body. Muscle meat is the mainstay of the Zombie Diet Plan. Muscles such as the biceps, quadriceps and pectorals are very well known but some of the most nutritious muscles are found deep in the body. The heart organ is actually a muscle that pumps blood around the body and is a good source of iron. It can be found in the centre of the chest cavity. You should eat it while it is still pumping to enjoy it at its freshest. Another good choice is the tongue, which is made up of very nutritious muscle meat. This sense organ, which deals with taste is a very tender meat and is high in vitamin B12, sodium potassium and selenium. The tongue has a pinkish colour and is located in the mouth. Bite it with your teeth and pull it out.

Tripe

Tripe is another name for stomach lining, although intestinal lining is also called by this name. It has a rubbery texture and can be a little difficult to 'stomach' at first, but it is abundant in the human body. The small intestine is covered with circular mucosal folds and projections called villi giving it a very large surface area. If the small intestine is laid out flat, its surface is roughly 250 square meters – the length of a tennis court! That's a lot of food. Intestines are quite easy to pull out through the abdominal wall. It may be a good idea to wash them out before eating.

Kidneys

Kidneys are considered a delicacy. They have a good supply of protein and are low in fat. They are also a good source of the B vitamins – riboflavin, pantothenic acid and niacin and contain various minerals - selenium, zinc, iron and calcium. Kidneys are delicious and a natural health-giving food. It is best to eat them as fresh as possible.

Lungs

These respiratory organs are located on either side of the upper chest. Lungs can be used in recipes to make haggis - a savoury pudding made of heart, liver and lungs encased in the stomach. They have good protein content and are low in fat. Lungs have a spongy texture.

One of the difficulties for zombies is in getting enough vitamin C, which strengthens the immune system. A deficiency in vitamin C can cause scurvy, a condition where the teeth become weak and your gums bleed. As zombies depend so much on having strong teeth, scurvy can be a disaster for zombies. Fortunately lungs are very high in vitamin C.

Liver

The liver has many functions in the human body, such as metabolism, detoxification and digestion. It is a large reddish brown organ with four lobes and is found in the right upper part of the abdomen. The liver has a soft meaty texture and is highly nutritious. Many human bodybuilders will often take desiccated animal liver supplements because they are high in protein. Liver also contains an abundance of vitamin A and several B vitamins, including folic acid and iron. It is one of the ultimate 'superfoods'. When many zombies are hunting a human together, there may often be a fight over who gets to eat the liver. It is at times like this, where all your training and physical conditioning will come in handy as you may have to fight another zombie in order to win this delicacy.

Sweetbread

This is another name for the thymus and pancreas organs. The thymus is an organ in the centre of the chest which is part of the immune system. The pancreas is a glandular organ which secretes hormones that assist in digestion. Despite the name, sweetbread is not sugary, but these meats do have a sweeter taste than other meats in the body. Sweetbread is high in protein and fat. The thymus is a pinkish meat with a wet texture and can be a little bit fiddly to eat as it is surrounded by a thick membrane, which may need to be peeled away before eating.

Chapter 9

The Zombie Plan Diet Compared to Other Diets

Bookshops are inundated with diet and fitness books - *low carbs, low fat, high fibre, vegetarian, macrobiotics, raw-foodism, food combining* and many more. A celebrity will endorse a diet one year and a completely different one the next. For the average person on the street, it can be very confusing to find the plan that fits you. Obviously if you've read this far, you will probably realise by now that the Zombie Exercise and Diet Plan is a superior program. However, just to give you a balanced view, I will talk about some other well-known diets and how they compare to the Zombie Plan. As there are so many diets to choose from, I will only pick those that are similar.

The Atkins diet

This is a very popular diet and is often referred to as a low carbohydrate, high protein diet. The Atkins diet advises you to reduce significantly your intake of carbohydrates, which causes the body to switch from metabolizing glucose for energy over to converting stored body fat to energy. This process is called ketosis.

When the body is in ketosis, you tend to feel less hungry, and are likely to eat less.   As you burn fat, you will lose weight. Unfortunately, ketosis can also cause a variety of unpleasant effects - bad breath, constipation, nausea and irritability.

In many ways the Zombie Diet is similar to the Atkins diet. The Zombie Diet *also* promotes a low carbohydrate diet with high levels of protein. However, the focus is not on losing weight but on getting fit! This is a key premise and is why the Atkins diet ultimately fails. The zombie diet is much more than a diet plan. It is a lifestyle plan. It doesn't matter what ratio of carbohydrates, protein or fat that you eat. If your energy expenditure is lower than your calorie intake, you will put on weight. The original Atkins diet did not promote exercise as part of the plan. In the Zombie Diet, the expenditure of energy is very high because you must hunt and chase your food. This burns a lot of energy. Also the exercises in the zombie plan help to increase metabolism and turns your body into a lean mean energy-converting machine. If you want to lose weight, you would be more successful following the Zombie Plan.

The Eskimo diet

Many mainstream human diet books usually promote the reduction of calories with varying ratios of the consumption of carbohydrates, proteins and fats.

However, nearly all diet plans agree on one thing: that fibre is absolutely essential for your health.

The Eskimo diet, also known as the 'Inuit' diet provides an interesting paradox. The Eskimo diet is almost entirely meat and fat based with no fibre and is extremely low in carbohydrates. Despite this, it has sustained the lives of the Inuit people in the Arctic for many generations. Inuit people even have lower cases of heart disease and cancer compared to other Western countries.

The main diet of the Inuit is seal, walrus, moose, caribou and reindeer meat along with fish and crabs that live in cold water. They typically use seal oil for cooking. These animals have high levels of fat to preserve them from the cold. This diet is good because it is packed full of essential nutrients. Vitamin A, D and the B vitamins are present in the oil of cold-water fish and in animal's livers. Vitamin C is found in caribou liver, whale skin and seal brain. Inuits also drink seal blood, which is believed to rejuvenate the blood of the drinker. This diet is said to make the Inuit people warmer, stronger and full of power.

The principles of the Inuit diet are exactly the same as the Zombie Diet. The Inuit get their nutrition from one food group – animal meat. The zombies also get their nutrition from one food group – humans. Even though they don't eat vegetables or fruit, neither the Inuit nor zombies suffer from vitamin or mineral deficiencies. This is because they are able to get these nutrients from other mammals that have eaten and digested various plant-life.

But in the end, the zombie diet is more effective. The Inuit diet can only be followed in the Arctic, where seal, fish and caribou are in abundance. Such a diet cannot work in city areas, as these animals do not live there (except in the zoo in small numbers). The zombie diet follows the same principles as the Inuit diet but is more effective because humans are in greater abundance all over the world.

The Paleo diet

The Paleo diet is also known as the caveman or hunter gatherer diet. It is based on the caveman diet of wild animals and plants from the palaeolithic era around 2.5 million years ago. The reasoning behind the diet is that humans are more adapted genetically and physiologically to these foods. The Palaeolithic diet consists of eating proteins, fats and small amounts of carbohydrates. Meat can be eaten raw or cooked.

In principle, the diet can be very effective. However, it is quite difficult to follow the diet authentically as it is very hard to match the conditions of the paleo-world in the modern world.   Proponents of the diet have made modern day adaptations to the diet by introducing foods like wholegrain wheat, brown rice and milk into the diet.

These would not have been available in the palaeolithic era and has made the diet less faithful to its ideals.

The diet itself is a form of lifestyle. To practice the Paleo diet in its true form would require hunting for wild animals and not using domesticated livestock from the supermarket. The physical action involved in hunting is the most important factor missing in the modern version although some humans attempt to substitute this activity by going to the gym and working out before eating.

In truth, the Zombie Diet incorporates the principles of the Paleo diet and is more practical. A zombie must hunt for its meat much like our cavemen ancestors did millions of years ago and eat their meals raw without flavouring or sauces.

The Okinawa diet

The Okinawa diet may also be called the 'long life' diet. It is a nutrient-rich, low-calorie diet eaten by the indigenous people of the Ryukyu Islands in Japan who have one of the highest life expectancy rates in the world. The diet consists of small quantities of white rice, or sweet potato and small amounts of fish. The Okinawans have very low mortality rates caused by cardiovascular disease and low levels of prostate and colon cancer compared to other Western countries. One of the key principles of the Okinawa diet is known as 'hara hachi bunme'. This is a Confucian teaching which roughly translates as "eat until your belly is 80% full". This concept has been supported by scientific research which shows that a significantly calorie restricted diet (eating small amounts) can actually prolong life.

In essence the diet is based on sound principles and the main selling point of the diet is that it is promoted by people with some of the longest life-spans in the world.

However, zombies survive much longer than Okinawans. In fact they may be considered immortal as once they become 'undead' they cannot die in the traditional sense *(unless killed by a shot to the head)*. This fact alone shows that the Zombie Diet is far superior.

FAQs

What does human meat taste like?

Human meat has its own distinct taste. If you wanted to compare it to animal meat, it has been described as a mild tasting meat similar to veal.   Of course, if you eat a human that has eaten a high junk food diet, the meat is likely to taste a little salty and oily.

Do I need to be infected by the zombie virus, before I start the plan?

You can if you want to be authentic, although it really isn't necessary. You can follow the plan and enjoy the benefits without actually becoming a zombie.

I've never hunted a human before. What's it like?

It's really no different to hunting any other animal like a deer or rabbit. Of course, if you've never hunted before, it can be quite challenging, so it's a good idea to join a club and go hunting together until you are confident to hunt by yourself. In every town and city there are usually many zombie hunting packs and associations you can join.

Won't my friends and family think I'm strange for changing to the Zombie Diet?

Probably, but then change can be scary for people to accept. You have to ask yourself: what's important to me? Do I want to please other people or do I want to enjoy greater levels of fitness and vitality? I can assure you that once they see the results, they will probably want to try the Zombie Plan out themselves.

I find it hard to eat raw meat? Can't I cook it a little?

It is often hard at first to eat raw meat, but persevere. After the first few weeks, you will find your body will get used to it and soon you won't be able to eat cooked meats at all without feeling sick.

What about organic meat? Is this best for me?

In an ideal world, we would all eat organic food. Unfortunately, in the case of organic food, some compromises have to be taken. Organic food is usually a lot more expensive and more difficult to find. Organic human meat is usually only found in wealthy health-conscious people: for example - in models and celebrities and therefore is in short supply. As the average human will contain varying amounts of antibiotics and pesticides, organic eating is really not worth the effort. It's better to aim to eat mostly free-range instead.

I still crave carbohydrates - especially buns and chocolate. How can I reduce these cravings?

You can do this simply by increasing your intake of human flesh. You are probably experiencing nutritional deficiencies. I suggest you get more fat in your diet. Good sources are the brain and liver. Pretty soon, those cravings will disappear.

Should I hunt other zombies or humans that are followers of the Zombie Plan?

The straightforward answer is no. If we look at zombies, we can see that they never eat their own. Humans are generally more technically competent and have many resources at their disposal to protect themselves such as weapons and armoured vehicles. It is essential for zombies to work together to overpower humans by sheer weight of number. This is why it's not in a zombie's best interests to hunt each other. Likewise, when following the diet, we also should work together with other followers of the zombie plan and make clubs and hunting packs.

My doctor says it's a crazy diet and is morally wrong. But I want to get fit. What should I do?

It's a sad state of affairs, but many physicians are not trained in nutrition and have only a very basic understanding of dietetics. Fortunately, thanks to patient's testimonies, more and more doctors are starting to recognise the benefits of the Zombie Exercise and Diet Plan. There is also a lot of ongoing research into this remarkable new breakthrough diet and fitness plan. Unfortunately, it will be many years before this diet is accepted in mainstream science. Do you really want to wait years to enjoy the benefits of the Zombie Plan? Thousands of people say no. And that is why the Ultimate Zombie Exercise and Diet Plan has changed the lives of so many.

The Final Word

By now you may realize that The Zombie Exercise and Diet plan is more than just a health program. It is a way of life. The Zombie Plan asks you to look at the way you live and the foods you eat. It asks you to evaluate certain lifestyle habits that have actually been damaging your health up to now. It asks you to make the Zombie Plan an integral part of your daily life – no different to brushing your teeth or putting on clothes. Only then can truly authentic results be achieved.

Health books often have the ability to momentarily inspire you to start a new lifestyle program with great gusto. You feel fired up and want to start those new exercises and eat those special foods immediately. However, by the second or third week that book is gathering dust on your shelf and you are back to your old habits. The Zombie Plan intends to be a more meaningful and longer lasting part of your life. But to do that often requires some internal changes: in particular, eradicating the resistance of change.

Some of the real problems in life we must deal with are fear and lack of self-confidence. The Zombie Plan is unique in that it requires you to change your habits into doing things that are not socially acceptable to many humans. This requires a lot of self-belief.

Many people fail to succeed in this plan because of social pressure and from fear of non-conformity. They fear what their parents, family, friends, neighbours, work colleagues and what even the stranger on the street will think about them. And yet people will stubbornly hold on to unhappiness and stress because change and the unknown is scary.

Change means death – the death of an old way of life. The zombies do not fear death nor change, and this is their greatest strength. If we can destroy the fear of change and of conformity to societal norms, our lives too can be more fulfilling, rewarding and healthier. If you have read this book to the end, then you too are ready for change. It is now time to go out and practice the Zombie Exercise and Diet Plan.

The Ultimate Zombie Exercise & Diet Book

The End

8711265R00090

Printed in Great Britain
by Amazon.co.uk, Ltd.,
Marston Gate.